Voices of the Past
Volume II

By Kaye England

Kaye England Publications
1017 West Main Street
Carmel, Indiana 46032
317-844-3636

Special Thanks to:

Mary Ellen Hopkins for all her encouragement, support, friendship and for sharing her great piecing techniques.

Anne Gallo and Susan Raban for their friendship and assistance in researching Lucretia Mott, Abigail Adams and Louisa May Alcott and for sharing their beautiful quilts.

Kevin Britton for his fabulous technical work on this book.

Caryl Schuetz for her beautiful photography.

Holice Turnbow of The Stencil Company for stencil designs honoring these women.

Leona Berg, Alice Cunningham, Melissa Taylor, Cathy Franks and Cecelia Purciful for their quilting expertise on my quilts.

Richard Friedman and Roy Frym of South Sea Imports for believing in me and for their wonderful fabric.

The Sales staff of South Sea Imports who promote my fabric line.

David Hopkins for his friendship and assistance in production of this book.

Aimee E. Newell, Nantucket Historical Society for research assistance on Lucretia Mott's quilt.

A'Lelia Bundles for sharing photographs of her great-great-grandmother, Madam C.J. Walker.

Women's History Network, Windsor, California for celebrating women.

Photographs are from the Library of Congress or in author's private collection unless otherwise credited.

Clipart images courtesy of Zedcor, Tucson, Arizona

The quiltmakers who generously share their quilts for this book.

My loyal staff at Quilt Quarters: Terri Gunn, Laurie Keller, Judy Pleiss, Caryl Schuetz, Alice Cunningham, Melissa Taylor; Peggy McKinney, Kathy Gwinn, Sally Wycoff, Cindy Sochar, Cyndia Gerner, Dian Himes, Diane Gladstone, Beverly Brewington, Laurie Barnett, Lorraine Rush and Judy Alvis for carrying on and keeping things in perspective as I finished my work.

First Printing 1998. ISBN 0-929950-24-0

Graphic design and layout by Kevin Britton of Great Britton Graphics, Indianapolis, Indiana

Photography by Caryl Schuetz, Indianapolis, Indiana.

Published by Kaye England Publications,
1017 West Main Street, Carmel, Indiana 46032, 317-844-3636

Table of Contents

"Light tomorrow with today."
Elizabeth Barett Browning

Living the Legacy

By Kaye England using fabrics from the "Voices of the Past" collection by Kaye England for South Sea Imports. Quilted by Cecelia A. Purciful
78" x 84"

I want to say something to all of you
who have become a part
of the fabric of my life.

The color and texture
which you have brought into my being
have become a song
and I want to sing it forever.

There is an energy in us
which makes things happen
when the paths of other persons
touch ours
and we have to be there
and let it happen.

When the time
of our particular sunset comes
our thing, our accomplishment
won't really matter a great deal.

But the clarity and care
with which we have loved others
will speak with vitality
of the great gift of life
we have been for each other.

Excerpt from the song, "Wherever You Go"
The Benedictine Foundation of the State of Vermont, Inc.,
Weston, Vermont. Composer, Gregory Norbet, O.S.B.

Dedication

Chelsea Kaye Richards
June 12, 1988

Morgan Taylor Richards
December 10, 1990

Brylie Shea England
March 19, 1993

Sydney Grace Richards
February 1, 1996

**To my beautiful granddaughters,
may you touch the future as you have touched me.
Love, Nana**

Introduction

Adesire to continue studying women of our past has guided me in this project as I have been persistent in learning as much as possible about our foremothers.

I have chosen twelve women of historical significance to honor with an original quilt block and story. This selection includes First Ladies: Abigail Adams, Grace Coolidge, Eleanor Roosevelt and Jacqueline Kennedy Onassis; Authors: Harriet Beecher Stowe and Louisa May Alcott; Social Reformers: Julia Ward Howe, Lucretia Mott and Susan B. Anthony; Abolitionist: Sojourner Truth; Businesswoman: Madam C.J. Walker; and Humanitarian: Helen Keller. Studying each woman, I discovered the circumstances that fashioned their lives and with this information tried to understand how our lives might be connected. I believe that understanding where we came from motivates us to pursue the dedication to causes undertaken by our foremothers and to celebrate the fact that as women we are carriers of this vast legacy.

In addition to the twelve original blocks, I have included traditional blocks giving you a wealth of quilt designs and piecing options. I selected names for the alternate blocks that connected them to women, but maybe not the name most widely recognized by quilters. Quilt blocks are known by many names, depending on region and time period. You'll find great fun in searching for optional names to your favorite blocks. The blocks and their stories should provide many hours of enjoyable reading and piecing.

My hope is that those reading this will be inspired in some way to proceed with their own research and we can continue to write women back into history for future generations.

"Far away there in the sunshine are my highest aspirations. I may not reach them, but I can look up and see their beauty, believe in them, and try to follow where they lead."
Louisa May Alcott

Preface

When I finished the first volume of **Voices of the Past**, I was quickly aware that there were many more famous women whose stories needed to be told, so I immediately began work. Now, four years later, this volume is nearing completion. As I began my selection of women, I found enough to do ten books, but was finally able to decide on the twelve women that I am proud to present.

A work of this magnitude could not be possible without the help of many wonderful friends and also the complete support of my family. I can never thank them enough for all their assistance and encouragement.

There have been many important women in my life and I've certainly been influenced by many more that all make me proud to be a woman. My mother was a constant source of inspiration for me and I hope she is proud. My daughter Sheila never ceases to amaze me as she nurtures and cares for her family and struggles to make the right decisions about the care and upbringing of her children. Her three girls Chelsea Kaye, Morgan Taylor and Sydney Grace are sure to make their mark in history. I also strongly admire my daughter-in-law Julie as she juggles her responsibilities at a full-time job with the care of her family. Her daughter Brylie Shea is certainly surrounded by strong role models. All the women in my life, aunts, cousins, nieces, sister-in-laws and friends are a dazzling collection of what makes women so powerful and wonderful. I cherish each and every one of them.

As I endeavor to honor women, I am careful to not overlook that the men in our life share in the joy of our own unique skills and talents as we pursue our dreams. My brother Ray is one of my biggest fans and is very important to me. Grandsons Austin and Nash are sure to be the type of men that will enhance the lives of all they touch. I am extremely proud of my son Bryan who has brought much joy into my life and is the model father and husband. My husband David has been enormously supportive of my work and has made it possible for me to continue, knowing I have his love. He is always available to listen to a story, photograph a quilt, keep the computer running, and yes to even cook dinner. I love you bunches.

All women have to continually struggle at building their self-esteem as they work in a society that generally has lower expectations of them. According to Susan Swartz, *"What's so amazing about women of the past who dared to succeed is that they overcame the prejudiced notion that women were never intended to do either – dare nor succeed."* It has been stated that Women's History is a treasure chest of stories of women's lives and accomplishments waiting to be discovered. May we all be diligent in this discovery!

The Women & Their Blocks

"... We learned to sew patchwork at school, while we were learning the alphabet; and almost every girl, large or small, had a bed-quilt of her own begun, with an eye to future house furnishing. I was not over fond of sewing, but I thought it best to begin mine early.

So I collected a few squares of calico, and undertook to put them together in my usual independent way, without asking direction. I liked assorting those little figured bits of cotton cloth, for they were scraps of gowns I had seen worn, and they reminded me of the persons who wore them."

Lucy Larcom
A New England Girlhood, 1889

Abigail Quincy Smith Adams

**1744 - 1818
Feminist,
First Lady**

"All talk of women's rights is moonshine. Women have every right. They have only to exercise them."
Victoria Woodhull

Abigail Quincy Smith was born November 11, 1744 in Weymouth, Massachusetts. Although a frail child, she survived the cold Massachusetts winters and all the other ills of infancy. Abigail was the offspring of four generations of New England Puritan preachers who was never sent to school because of her delicate condition, but she had an unlimited source of reading material at her disposal. She learned to read and write proficiently, became adept at spinning, weaving, soapmaking and all other household chores. Abigail was taught the skill of fancy sewing and was given the gift of her grandmother's love of laughter and virtue, teachings that remained with her throughout her life.

While Abigail was growing up in Weymouth, young John Adams was working on his father's farm at Braintree (now Quincy), near Weymouth. When they met, John had graduated from Harvard and was prac-

ticing law in his home district. At this time law was a new occupation many people thought to be a lazy profession so Abigail's family discouraged his attentions. Nineteen year old Abigail did not feel this way, and despite all objections, they were married October 25, 1764. As the sacred words were recited and vows pledged, Abigail and John were united with a love and devotion that would span over 50 years.

In the coming years Abigail was busy raising a family of five children. This witty and virtuous woman became a skilled farmer, political advisor, admired businesswoman, articulate letter writer, devoted wife and mother. Abigail and John were impassioned abolitionists early on and she was also a spirited feminist who gave this immortal advice to John;

"I desire that you remember the Ladies, and be more generous and favorable to them than your ancestors. Do not put such unlimited power into the hands of the Husbands. Remember all Men would be tyrants if they could. If particular care and attention is not paid to the Ladies we are determined to foment a Rebellion and we will not hold ourselves bound by any laws in which we have no voice or representation."

This gem of wisdom imparted to John is well remembered and certainly shows that even in the last quarter of the eighteenth century women were resisting domination. Most of her letters to John would begin *"Dearest Friend."* As they became equal partners in marriage, Abigail managed the family estate and reported on the events of the Revolutionary War during John's frequent absences. While John was away helping draft the constitution of this new nation, many believe that Abigail became a better statesman than her husband and was said to have influenced many decisions

Abigail Quincy Smith Adams

made by both husband and son during their presidencies. I find it interesting that during this period a First Lady had such a tremendous effect on the presidency as we seem to think these attributes belong only to the twentieth century.

While Abigail was tending the farm and raising their family, John was in Philadelphia working with men such as Patrick Henry, Lee, Washington and other leaders to unify against England. In the spring of 1775, with the war literally at their front door, John wrote to Abigail, *"In case of real danger... fly to the woods with our children."* Abigail replied; *"I would not have you distressed about me. Danger, they say, makes people valiant."* These are sure signs of a strong and determined woman. When the minutemen came to the farm, Abigail gave them her pewter spoons to be melted for bullets. When she joined John in England in 1784, she endured royal disdain and noted the tyranny of aristocracy. She was appalled by the lavish display and the pomp and pageantry that excluded the average citizen.

Before becoming the leader of this country, Adams was the vice-president under George Washington. When Adams was inaugurated as President in Philadelphia, the capital was moved to Washington where Abigail became the first First Lady to actually live in the White House. The new mansion was so large that Abigail used the East Room for drying clothes finding the task of managing this large structure quite difficult. She did begin to entertain more generously, believing that the presidency should carry the same dignity of the European courts. During this time colonial dancing was all the vogue and with the gentlemen all resplendent in their white wigs, brocade coats, silken breeches, and silver buckled shoes; and elegant ladies sparkling with jewels, in rustling gowns, high-heeled silk slippers and curled hair, they all enjoyed the minuet.

President John Adams was politically handicapped from the beginning, following the much loved George Washington, a man armed with all the personal charm and tact that Adams did not possess. Abigail understood the difficulties facing her husband and was relieved when at the end of his term in 1801 they could return to their beloved Braintree for more peaceful times. During these retirement years she kept busy tending the farm, caring for their home and writing letters to her son John Quincy Adams or Mr. JQA as she called him.

Abigail was extremely proud of Mr. JQA's rising importance but sadly she did not live to see him become President. She had acted as counsel and guide to two men who both became president of this great Nation. On October 28, 1818, with her husband by her side, this delightful woman quietly passed away. Her son John paid a most loving tribute to her memory;

"My Mother was an angel on earth. She has been more to me than a mother. She has been a spirit from above."

In remembering Abigail Adams, the insightful words with which she reassured her husband hold great significance:

"I have learned to know the world and its value, I have seen high life. I have witnessed the luxury and pomp of state, the power of riches, and the influence of titles. Notwithstanding this, I feel that I can return to my little cottage and be happier... and if we have not wealth, we have what is better - integrity."

"Wisdom and penetration are the fruit of experience, not the lessons of retirement and leisure. Great necessities call out great virtues."
Abigail Adams

Abigail Quincy Smith Adams

John Adams lived another eight years after Abigail's death, and in honor to a marriage of mutual love and respect spanning 54 years, her final resting place is beside her husband at United First Parish Church in Quincy, Massachusetts.

Abigail Adams was one of the early pioneers in founding our country and her way of life provides optimism and assurance to all women.

This most extraordinary spirit paved the way for a new generation of women. I designed this block in her honor, offering the dual stars to commemorate both her life and the numerous lives she inspired.

Remember The Ladies
By Kaye England & Friends
Quilted by Cathy Franks
56" x 63"

"These are the hard times in which a genius would wish to live. Great necessities call forth great leaders."
Abigail Adams

12

Abigail Quincy Smith Adams

**Abigail Adams
(12" Block)**

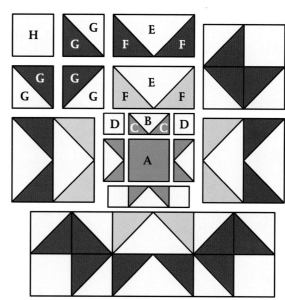

Piece	Fabric	Cut	/Yield	Cutting Instructions
A	Medium	1		2-1/2" square
B	Light	4		1-1/2 x 2-1/2" rectangles
C	Medium	8		1-1/2" square Connector Corners
D	Light	4		1-1/2" squares
E	Light	8		2-1/2 x 4-1/2" rectangles
F	Med-2	8		2-1/2" square Connector Corners
F	Dark	8		2-1/2" square Connector Corners
G	Light	6	12	2-7/8" squares cut into half-sq. triangles
G	Dark	6	12	2-7/8" squares cut into half-sq. triangles
H	Light	4		2-1/2" squares

Assemble block following piecing diagram above. See helpful instructions in Construction Tips & Advice. Connector Corners make this block a breeze.

"O' Morning Stars Together"
By Diane Gladstone of Carmel, Indiana
42" x 42"

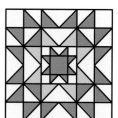

Optional colorings for this block!

Grace Anna Goodhue Coolidge

**1879-1957
First Lady,
Schoolteacher**

"*People are my favorite book.*"
Grace Coolidge

race Anna Goodhue was born on January 3, 1879 in Burlington Vermont, the only child of Lemira and Andrew Goodhue. Growing up in the Green Mountains, Grace heard of a school for deaf children in Northampton, Massachusetts, and decided this would become her vocation. She was educated at the University of Vermont moving to Northampton in 1902 to begin teaching at the Clark School for the Deaf.

Through a window next door Grace caught a glimpse of the man she would marry one day. She saw Calvin Coolidge shaving, clad only in long underwear and a derby hat, and broke out in laughter. Hearing her laugh, he was determined to meet her. Although they were two distinctly different natures, they were drawn to each other and married October 4, 1905.

They made their home in Northampton where Mr. Coolidge was elected mayor in 1910 and Grace busied herself raising their two young sons. The boys inherited Grace's sunny disposition and she became a model of domesticity, knitting, sewing, and keeping house for her family. They never discussed his work and she never tried to influence his decisions. Although he was a penny-pincher, he was extravagant in buying her clothes. He adored Grace and wanted her to appear at every affair in a different outfit.

Coolidge became Governor of Massachusetts and later vice-president. After the death of President Harding, he was sworn in as president during a midnight ceremony by his father Colonel John Coolidge. These sudden political responsibilities gave Grace her position as the First Lady where her attention and friendliness were spent enhancing the position. Whatever she might have learned of the nation's business she learned from newspapers and not from her husband, as she made no speeches and granted no interviews during their stay at the White House. Whistling her way through the days turned every affair into an occasion with her sincere, genuine welcoming smile, endearing her to the American people.

Sadness touched the first family in 1924, when their son Calvin, Jr., died from blood poisoning. This event influenced President Coolidge's decision not to run for a second term. Happy to return to Northampton, Grace worked for the Red Cross and served on the board of trustees at the Clark School for the Deaf.

They purchased a large house in Northampton where Calvin Coolidge died in 1933. He summed up their marriage in his Autobiography;

14

Grace Anna Goodhue Coolidge

"For almost a quarter of a century she has borne with my infirmities, and I have rejoiced in her graces."

After his death she traveled to Europe, took her first ride in an airplane and spent time with their son John and his family. She was a loyal Boston Red Sox fan and during World War II aided refugee children entering the United States. She was awarded a gold medal by the National Institute of Social Science for distinguished services both in behalf of her school work for the deaf and for personal influence exerted while she served as First Lady of the Nation.

Grace Anna Goodhue Coolidge died of a heart attack on July 8, 1957 and was laid to rest beside Calvin Coolidge in Plymouth, Vermont. She had left a will expressing her wish that President Coolidge's birthplace be turned over to the state of Vermont and by the end of the year her wishes had been fulfilled.

On the dedication of President Coolidge's birthplace, President Eisenhower remembered Grace Coolidge with this message:

"It is a matter of profound sorrow to all Americans that the beloved Mrs. Grace Coolidge could not have lived to

Simply Grace
By Kaye England
Quilted by Cathy Franks
50" x 60"

"The Whitehouse is a home rich in tradition, mellowed with years, hallowed with memories."
Grace Coolidge

15

participate in the dedication of this home which held so many happy memories for her. In setting aside this memorial, she might well have used her husband's own words: 'Men build monuments above the graves of their heroes to mark the end of a great life; but women seek out the birthplace and build their shrines not where a great life had its ending but where it had its beginning; seeking with a truer instinct the common source of things, not in that which is gone forever but in that which they know will again be manifest. Life may depart, but the source of life is constant."

This simple star block is in honor of the simplicity and dignity in which Grace Coolidge lived her life.

Above:
Grace Coolidge
By Anne Gallo of Chelmsford, Massachusetts & Susan Raban of Nashua, New Hampshire
40" x 40"

Right:
Grace Coolidge
By Dian Himes of Brownsburg, Indiana
64" x 64"

Grace Anna Goodhue Coolidge

**Grace Coolidge
(12" Block)**

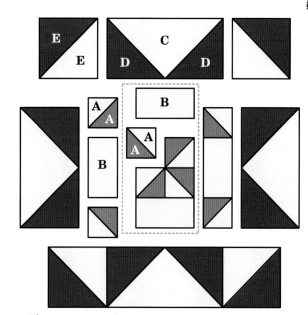

Piece	Fabric	Cut	Yield	Cutting Instructions
A	Light	4	8	2-3/8" sq. cut into half-square triangles
A	Dark	4	8	2-3/8" sq. cut into half-square triangles
B	Light	4		2 x 3-1/2" rectangles
C	Light	4		3-1/2 x 6-1/2" rectangles
D	Medium	8		3-1/2" sq. Connector Corners
E	Medium	2	4	3-7/8" sq. cut into half-square triangles
E	Light	2	4	3-7/8" sq. cut into half-square triangles

Assemble block following piecing diagram above. See helpful piecing instructions in Construction Tips & Advice. Connector Corners are used to simplify construction of this block.

Enduring Grace
*By Marianne Roan of
Indianapolis, Indiana
32" x 32"*

During the Coolidge term, Grace crocheted a bedspread for the huge Lincoln bed. Allotting one month for each square in the spread, she stitched off a month in the Coolidge tenure as she completed the spread.

Anna Eleanor Roosevelt

**1884-1962
Writer,
Diplomat,
Humanitarian
& First Lady**

"No one can make you feel inferior without your consent."
Eleanor Roosevelt

Anna and Elliot Roosevelt, became the proud parents of their firstborn child Anna Eleanor Roosevelt on October 11, 1884. Named for her mother Anna, it was decided the baby would be called Eleanor and a life began that would span seventy-eight years and touch millions of people.

Eleanor's early memory unveils a cheerless childhood as her mother referred to her as a *"funny child"*, or called her *"granny"* because she was so old fashioned and unattractive. The fact that this painfully shy and awkward child possessed poor posture and protruding teeth only added to her sense of inadequacy. It's ironic in a family of this gentility and affluence that such unkindness would be shed on this sensitive child. Her father was the only person she was able to love without any reserve and she many times called him *"the love of my life."* He fondly referred to her as his *"Little Nell."*

She lost her mother at the age of eight, her father was then not deemed able to raise a child, so she was sent to live with her Grandmother Hall, a stern woman who also let Eleanor know how unattractive she was. Two years later Eleanor lost her father and life seemed to have no significance. Grandmother Hall hoped with hours of dance designed to improve her balance, braces for her teeth, braces for her rounded shoulders and strict discipline, Eleanor would gain self-confidence and improved manners. Her real personality began to unfold when she was sent to England at the age of fifteen. With self-determination and the friendship of a teacher, Eleanor began to blossom and realized that if she would place her concerns on those around her, she could indeed lead a useful and happy life. This deep felt kindness for others would remain with her through her life.

When Eleanor returned to New York at the age of eighteen, her aunt remarked that as an "ugly duckling" she would never find a beau. The handsome young Franklin Roosevelt, a distant cousin, appreciated this plain young lady and they married on March 17, 1905, with the bride given in marriage by her Uncle Theodore Roosevelt.

Knowing little about running a household or raising children, married life was a difficult adjustment for Eleanor. Franklin's mother lived with them and assumed all the responsibility of the household, enabling Eleanor's lack of self-confidence to return. Their marriage produced six children in ten years, and when Franklin was elected senator in 1910, Eleanor finally began what would be her new life. By the time we entered World War I, Eleanor was an experienced hostess, and had become in-

Anna Eleanor Roosevelt

volved in the work of war. She devoted time to Red Cross activities, served meals, visited hospitals and many days worked from morning until midnight in this service.

Eleanor faced her toughest challenge in 1921, when Franklin was stricken with polio while on vacation. Supported by his wife and his mother, Franklin fought for his life eventually regaining the use of his upper body but remained partially paralyzed the rest of his life.

Eleanor became interested in public affairs, she joined the Women's Trade Union, the League of Women Voters, organized women voters in New York, worked for child labor laws and drew attention to women's issues in the Democratic party. With all these new involvements it was necessary for her to make many public speeches. Eleanor was quoted as saying;

"I suppose inwardly I'm still shy and dislike talking and appearing in public. I don't think anyone ever gets over that, really, but I might say I can now control my feelings and hide my inward shyness so that outwardly I appear calm and unafraid."

Public speaking was only one of the hurdles Eleanor was to overcome as she learned to swim, drive a car and became both mother and father to the children.

In 1928, Franklin Roosevelt became governor of New York. Eleanor became immersed in a career of public service supporting her husband in every way. When in 1933 the White House became their home, Eleanor was seasoned in her role and began touring the country on missions of interest to her husband, talking on the radio, and writing a syndicated column, *"My Day,"* for a newspaper. She continued her travels during the sec-

ond World War, reporting back to the President with regularity. This should reaffirm even in the first half of this century, that a First Lady could become the center of criticism, enduring hostile writings, jokes and mockeries of her appearance while ignoring claims that she had too great an influence over the President.

On January 20, 1945, President Roosevelt was inaugurated for a record fourth time while we were still at war. On April 12, 1945, Franklin Delano Roosevelt died of a massive cerebral hemorrhage at Warm Springs, Georgia. Eleanor continued her duties and began the sad task of contacting the children and important dignitaries around the world. She was present when Harry Truman took the oath of office as the thirty-third President of the United States.

At seventy-five, Eleanor began a new career, lecturing at Brandeis University, she also taped a television commercial for margarine. The decision to do this was made clearer when she determined that with the $35,000 fee paid for the commercial, she could purchase many CARE packages. Knowing there would be protests, Eleanor once again put the needs of others over her own feelings. She stated;

"The mail was evenly divided, with one half sad because I had damaged my reputation and the other half happy because I had damaged my reputation."

She continued to remain active in politics serving on the Tractors for Freedom Committee, and the Advisory Council of the Peace Corps during President Kennedy's administration. Her warmth and sensitivity was shared with Jacqueline Kennedy when she wrote her the following note;

"I suppose I should slow down, I think I have a good deal of my Uncle Theodore in me, because I could not, at any age, be content to take my place in a corner by the fireside and simply look on. Life was meant to be lived. Curiosity must be kept alive. The fatal thing is the rejection. One must never, for whatever reason, turn his back on life."
Eleanor Roosevelt

19

Eleanor Roosevelt
By Elizabeth Lake of Kingston, Ontario, Canada 34" x 34"

"A woman is like a teabag, you never know how strong it is until it's in hot water."
Eleanor Roosevelt

"I know that there will be difficulties in store for you in the White House life but perhaps also you will find some compensations. Most things are made easier, though I think on the whole life is rather difficult for both the children and their parents in the 'fish bowl' that lies before you."

They continued a warm friendship with Mrs. Roosevelt being very happy this young couple and their children were living in her former home.

Matriarch to twenty grandchildren and many great-grandchildren, Eleanor spent her last years enjoying shopping trips for Christmas, entertaining at Hyde Park, telling stories of her childhood and sharing special times with friends. She particularly was pleasured when her own grandchildren shared her interests and values.

On November 7, 1962 Eleanor Roosevelt's strong heart ceased to beat and the words she had spoken on Edward R. Murrow's program, were remembered:

"This I Believe, I believe that all that you go through here must have some value, therefore there must be some reason. And there must be some "going on". How exactly that happens I've never been able to decide. There is a future that I'm sure of: But how, that I don't know. And I came to feel that it didn't really matter very much because whatever the future held you'd have to face it when you came to it, just as whatever life holds you have to face it in exactly the same way. And the important thing was that you never let down doing the best that you were able to do — it might be poor because you might not have much within you to give, or to help other people with, or to live your life with. But as long as you did the very best that you were able to do, then that was what you were put here to do and that was what you were accomplishing by being here. And so I have tried to follow that out - and not to worry about the future or what was going to happen. I think I am pretty much of a fatalist. You have to accept whatever comes and the only important thing is that you meet it with courage and with the best that you have to give!"

Eleanor was laid to rest at Hyde Park, having been nominated for, but never receiving the Nobel Peace Prize. To an entire nation she had earned this distinction as well as their everlasting devotion and admiration.

I remember the outpouring of love shared by a nation when Eleanor Roosevelt passed away and have been in awe of her contributions and the manner in which she lived her life. The star in this block represents the shining light of her determination and the solid path around the star represents the warmth of her spirit as it enveloped the world. I believe Anna Eleanor Roosevelt's noble spirit will live forever, inspiring future generations to follow in her footsteps.

Anna Eleanor Roosevelt

**Eleanor Roosevelt
(12" Block)**

Piece Fabric Cut/Yield Cutting Instructions

Piece	Fabric	Cut	Yield	Cutting Instructions
A	Light	1	4	2-3/4" sq. cut into quarter-square triangles
A	Medium	1	4	2-3/4" sq. cut into quarter-square triangles
B	Light	12	24	2-3/8" sq. cut into half-square triangles
B	Medium	2	4	2-3/8" sq. cut into half-square triangles
B	Dark	8	16	2-3/8" sq. cut into half-square triangles
C	Light	12		2 x 3-1/2" rectangles
C	Dark	8		2 x 3-1/2" rectangles
D	Light	16		2" square Connector Corners
D	Medium	8		2" square Connector Corners
D	Dark	16		2" square Connector Corners

Assemble block following piecing diagram above. See helpful piecing instruction in Construction Tips & Advice. Quick piecing techniques are used to simplify construction of this block.

Eleanor Roosevelt (Table Runner)
By Laurie Barnett of Carmel, Indiana
In the collection of Marcia Altic
24" x 64"

Eleanor's Eulogy

Fabric Yardages

Black print	1-3/4 yards
Assorted Reds	2 yards
Assorted Backgrounds	1-3/4 yards
Backing/Binding	4 yards

Center Medallion

Create four Eleanor Roosevelt blocks following instructions on previous page (see photo on page 23 for color placement). Use a variety of reds and background prints (tan) to create a "scrappy" look.

Border One

Cut the following:

Black print 2 2-1/2 x 24-1/2" strips
Black print 2 2-1/2 x 28-1/2" strips
Attach short strips to sides, then attach longer ones to top and bottom. Make sure everything is square after each row.

Border Two

Using reds and background fabrics make sixty half-square triangle units. Cut 30 2-7/8" squares from each light and dark fabric, cut diagonally into two triangles, join one red to one background triangle to create a 2"finished square. Make four strips of fourteen of these units and attach one each to the sides. Add additional units to the ends of the remaining strips and attach these to top and bottom.

Half-Square Triangle Units

Border Three

Cut the following:

Black print 2 2-1/2 x 32-1/2" strips
Black print 2 2-1/2 x 36-1/2" strips
Attach short strips to sides and longer strips to top and bottom.

"Friendship with oneself is all important, because without it one cannot be friends with anyone else in the world."
Eleanor Roosevelt

Border Four

Again, using reds and background prints make forty quarter-square triangle units. Cut twenty 5-1/4" squares out of each fabric, place a red and background fabric right-sides together, mark diagonal line on lighter fabric and sew 1/4" on each side of line. Cut on center line and press open to form squares. Take two of these units (randomly), place the right-sides together matching opposite colors to each other and make sure center seams align with each other (see illustration). Again, mark a diagonal line crosswise from the center seam and stitch 1/4" on each side of this line, cut apart and press open (see illustration).

Quarter-Square Triangle Units (Scrappy)

Border Five

Cut the following

Black print 2 2-1/2 x 44-1/2" strips
Black print 2 2-1/2 x 48-1/2" strips
Attach short strips to sides and longer strips to top and bottom.

Eleanor's Eulogy

Border Six

Using Connector Corners make fifty-two Dugout squares out of the two fabrics. Cut fifty-two 4-1/2" red squares and 104 2-1/2" background Connector Corner squares. Lay a small square right-sides together on opposite corners of a large square and sew diagonally across each, trim background fabric only and press back to form finished squares (assemble following diagram).

Trim Connector Corner only! Press & Fold.

Dugout Units (Connector Corners)

Border Seven

Cut the following:
Black print   2   2-1/2 x 56-1/2" strips
Black print   2   2-1/2 x 60-1/2" strips
Attach short strips to sides and longer strips to top and bottom.

Finishing

See helpful instructions in the Construction Tips & Advice section of this book to "sandwich" and quilt your new project.

Eleanor's Eulogy
*By Kaye England
Quilted by Cathy
Franks
60" x 60"*

"Whoever is happy will make others happy too."
Anne Frank

23

Jacqueline Lee Bouvier Kennedy Onassis

**1929-1994
First Lady,
Editor**

"What is sad for a woman of my generation is that they weren't suppose to work if they had families. What were they to do when the children were grown... watch the raindrops coming down the window pane?"
Jacqueline Onassis

Jacqueline Lee was born on July 28, 1929 to the wealthy and socially prominent Bouvier family of Southampton, Long Island, New York. She was educated in the finest private schools where she studied ballet, drew illustrations for the stories and poems that she wrote and became a photo journalist after graduating in 1951.

While working at the Washington Times-Herald one of her interviews was with the handsome John Kennedy where a romance resulted and culminated in a wedding that was the social event of the year in September 1953. Jacqueline Kennedy was determined to be the 'perfect' wife and settled into the whirlwind life of a public figure. Her life was touched by tragedy early with two miscarriages and the delicate back surgeries endured by her husband. She at last found a sense of purpose and security with the birth of daughter Caroline in 1957 and son John in 1960. Jacqueline was a natural born mother, preferring to spend time with her children than beating the campaign trail with her husband. The approaching election involved her in the political arena forever earning her the respect and admiration of the Kennedy family and an entire nation.

Jacqueline Kennedy swept down on the White House like a fresh spring breeze and set about to bring dignity and grace to John Kennedy's presidency. She was the recipient of acclaim and awards, such as Woman of the Year, Ten Best Dressed Women list and began to enhance the historic atmosphere of the White House. During this time she fiercely guarded their privacy and that of her children.

Even though still saddened by the death of their young son Patrick in August 1963, they left on the historic Dallas trip. On November 22, 1963 the true meaning of faith and dignity was demonstrated when her beloved John was killed by an assassin's bullets as she sat beside him. President John Kennedy was pronounced dead at 1:00 PM on that fateful day, but it was reported he breathed his last in the arms of his wife on the way to the hospital. The hours and days that followed, a nation mourned the loss of their president, while a young widow grieved for her fallen husband. We were comforted as a nation by the grace and dignity with which the First Lady handled this last of her official duties. It was written by Katherine Porter;

"No one who witnessed that three-day funeral service, in presence or by screen, can ever say again that we, as a nation, cannot conduct the ceremonies of our state. We have been well taught. "

No one could have possibly done more than she on those sad days. She honored her husband, gave meaning

24

Jacqueline Lee Bouvier Kennedy Onassis

to his death and brought glory to the country they loved. A British writer said;

"She sustained a steel mind and an unbreakable will beneath the sweet surface of her gentle manner "

Jacqueline became the fourth First Lady to be widowed by an assassin. Mrs. Lincoln, Mrs. Garfield and Mrs. McKinley had endured the same tragic events. After the funeral she began to repair the torn threads of her life.

Shortly after her brother-in-law Robert Kennedy was killed, she married the wealthy Greek shipowner Aristotle Onassis much to the surprise of a nation thinking of her as Mrs. John F. Kennedy. This marriage offered her a secluded life and protection for her children, but ended with his death in March 1975.

"Wisp of Glory"
By Geneva Carroll of Rocklin, California
42" x 42"

"Stars for Jacqueline"
By Judy Pleiss of
Indianapolis, Indiana
48" x 48"

"No one else looked like her, spoke like her, wrote like her... no one we knew ever had a better sense of self... Jackie was too young to be a widow in 1963 and too young to die now. She was a part of our family and part of our hearts for forty wonderful and unforgettable years, and she will never really leave us."
Senator Ted Kennedy

Jacqueline Lee Bouvier Kennedy Onassis

From 1975 to 1977 she was consulting editor at Viking Press, moved to Doubleday in 1978 as an associate editor, later becoming a senior editor, working in her small book-filled office until a few weeks before her death.

The last years of her life were spent with the things she loved most, family, friends and work. She delighted in spending time with her grandchildren Rose, Tatiana and Jack, watching them grow and play. She also nurtured an unbelievable relationship with her children Caroline and John, strong in the belief that raising them as she had, was the best thing she had done. She stated;

"If you bungle raising your children, I don't think whatever else you do well matters very much."

Jacqueline Kennedy Onassis passed away on May 19, 1994, at her home in New York City with loved ones by her side. Thousands looked on at a distance during the funeral service at St. Ignatius Loyal church on Park Avenue. In 1963 Jackie had memorialized all that was good and true about her husband at his funeral, and her children Caroline and John sought the same thing for their mother. Her body was transported to Washington and laid to rest beside President Kennedy. President Clinton said:

"God gave her very great gifts and imposed upon her great burdens. She bore them all with dignity and grace and uncommon common sense."

She entered our lives like a fairytale princess, touched us deeply and gained our respect and love throughout her life. I designed this block to represent the time of "Camelot".

"Ask every person if he's heard the story... and tell it strong and clear if he has not.., that once there was a fleeting wisp of glory...called Camelot."

Camelot
By Dian Himes of Brownsburg, Indiana
52" x 52"

"If she taught us anything it was to know the meaning of responsibility - to one's family and to one's community. Her great gift of grace and style and dignity and heroism is an example that will live through the ages."
Hillary Clinton

Jacqueline Lee Bouvier Kennedy Onassis

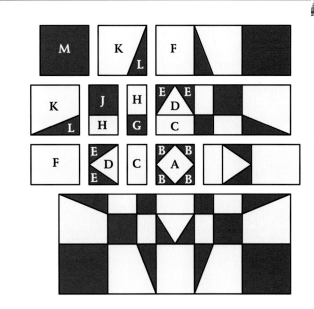

Jacqueline Kennedy
(12" Block)

Piece	Fabric	Cut/Yield	Quick Cut
A	Light	1	2-1/2" square
B	Dark	4	1-1/2" square Connector Corners
C	Light	4	2-1/2" x 1-1/2" rectangles
D	Light	4	2-1/2 x 2" rectangles
E	Dark	8	2 x 2-1/2" bias Connectors
F	Light	4	2-1/2 x 3" rectangles
G	Dark	4	1-1/2" squares
H	Light	8	1-1/2 x 2" rectangles
J	Dark	4	2" squares
K	Light	8	3" squares
L	Dark	8	2-1/2 x 3" bias Connectors
M	Dark	4	3" squares

Assemble block following drawing above. For pieces E and L see the instruction on Bias Rectangles in Construction Tips & Advice. Connector Corners are used in this block to simplify construction.

Place K and L right sides together. Mark on top edge 1/8" from the right-hand edge and on bottom edge 1-3/8" from the right-hand edge. Sew along a line connecting these two marks. Fold L back, press and trim. Reverse for mirror piece.

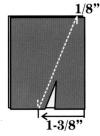

Gift of Grace
By Jan Krueger of Hales Corner, Wisconsin
24" x 24"

27

Lucretia Coffin Mott

1793 - 1880
Social
Reformer

"Man cannot fulfill his destiny alone, he cannot redeem his race unaided... The world has never yet seen a truly great and virtuous nation, because in the degradation of women the very foundations of life are poisoned at their source."
Lucretia Mott

Lucretia Coffin was born on January 3, 1793 in Nantucket, Massachusetts, the second daughter of Thomas Coffin, Jr., a Quaker sea captain and Anna Folger Coffin, a warm, strong woman who kept shop while her husband was at sea. Lucretia's life on Nantucket was mostly one of joy and the love of the island would remain with her throughout her life.

In accordance with her father's wish Lucretia attended public school in Boston for two years so that she would become familiar with the workings of the democratic principles. Lucretia's mother would have a profound effect on her entire life as Lucretia regularly called upon this deep love to see her through a crisis. Lucretia enrolled in a Friend's boarding school at Nine Partners near Poughkeepsie, New York and in a few short years went from student to teacher. During this time she was made painfully aware of the fact that even though women teachers were as experienced as their male counterparts they were not paid accordingly. This too would remain with her.

In April 1811, Lucretia married James Mott, a fellow teacher at Nine Partners and they settled into married life welcoming their first child in 1812. In the spring of 1818 Lucretia began speaking at religious meetings and a few years later was accepted as a minister of the Friends. When asked years later by one of her grandchildren why she became a preacher, she replied that the grief from the death of her young son had simply taken her mind that way. Lucretia joined the Hicksite branch of the society when a rift occurred in the 1820's and began traveling around the country lecturing on religion, social reform, temperance and the abolition of slavery. Although universal equality was her life's goal she was an advocate for religious reform and abhorred war above all.

Her involvement with women's rights began in 1840 when she and James were in London as delegates to the World's Anti-Slavery Convention. When she was refused admission based purely on her sex she became very upset about the discrimination. A meeting with Elizabeth Cady Stanton would alter her life. They decided to call a Woman's Rights Convention and held the first convention in Seneca Falls, New York in July 1848. The *"Declaration of Sentiments"* was language recalling the *"Declaration of Independence"* for equality before the law for women. They discussed and organized women across the country to fight the inequalities confronting them. Lucretia would remain an active participant in all these meetings through her eighty-sixth year.

Lucretia Coffin Mott

Lucretia and James opened their home to runaway slaves on the Underground Railroad route after the Fugitive Slave Law was adopted in 1850. Lucretia was a fluent and moving speaker who retained her poise and femininity before even the most hostile of crowds. After the Civil War she continued to be active in all causes of women's rights, peace and liberal religion. At the organizing meeting of the American Equal Rights Association in 1866 she was chosen president and in 1867 organized the Free Religious Association

James Mott died in 1868 with Lucretia and family by his side. Their fifty-six years of marriage were marked by love, devotion and mutual support and Lucretia stated that after his death hardly a day passed that she did not think of him and she never again slept in the wide marriage bed they had shared.

In 1876, after a reading of the **"Declaration of Sentiments"** at the First Unitarian Church, Lucretia rose to speak following the singing of the hymn, *"Nearer My God to Thee."* In response to many in the audience that were weeping Lucretia spoke;

"Weep not for me, rather let your tears flow for the sorrows of the multitude. My work is done. Like a ripe fruit I await the gathering. Death has no terrors, for it is a wise law of nature. I am ready whenever the summons may come."

This year would also be the last time Lucretia would visit her beloved Nantucket.

In 1878 she traveled to Seneca Falls for the thirtieth anniversary of the Women's Rights Convention and spoke at the convention saying;

"Give woman the privilege of cooperating in making the laws, and there will be harmony without severity, justice without oppression."

She received a standing ovation while many in the crowd realized this might be her last public appearance.

Lucretia remained close to home during the last few years of her life, surrounded by family and the simple daily pleasures of sewing, reading and gardening. The 1880 meeting of the Peace Society's Executive Committee was her last. She had requested a simple funeral service stating;

"Mine has been a simple life, let simplicity mark the last done for me. "

Lucretia Mott died in her sleep on November 11, 1880 and received the simple service she had requested. However thousands gathered at Fair Hill Cemetery in Philadelphia as a member of the Peace Society spoke. A silence then fell over the crowd as one man whispered, *"Will no one speak?"* Another replied, *"Who can speak ? The preacher is dead!"* She lies next to her beloved James, surrounded by her children and grandchildren open to *"heaven's light"* as she would have wished.

On a recent visit to Nantucket I had the privilege to 'visit' with a quilt made by Lucretia Mott that is in the care of the Nantucket Historical Association. Aimee E. Newell is registrar and shared this experience with my friends Anne, Susan and I during a documentation project. I was pleased to see that much of the quilt was simple triangles similar to the block I designed in her honor. In an excerpt from her book, **Discourse of Women - 1850**, she stated:

"Let women then go on - not asking as favour, but claiming as right, the removal of all the hindrances to her el-

"I learned long ago to lean on myself: "
Lucretia Mott

Lucretia Coffin Mott

evation in the sale of being - let her receive encouragements for the proper cultivation of all her powers, so that she may enter profitable into the active business of life; employing her own hands in ministering to her necessities, strengthening her physical being by proper exercise and observance of the laws of health."

Throughout her life, Lucretia Mott fought the conception of woman that defined woman as inferior to man. She truly believed in the principle of individual responsibility and that everyone should take action to correct the evils of the world. She prayed for the end of injustice and believed action was necessary if all were to attain happiness in their life. Her life was lived fighting to achieve equality for all. Lucretia Mott was a true crusader for peace.

"Declaration of Sentiments"
By Kaye England
Quilted by Alice Cunningham
44" x 44"

"Declaration of Sentiments"...
"We hold these truths to be self evident: That all men and women are created equal..."
Elizabeth Cady Stanton

Lucretia Coffin Mott

**Lucretia Mott
(12" Block)**

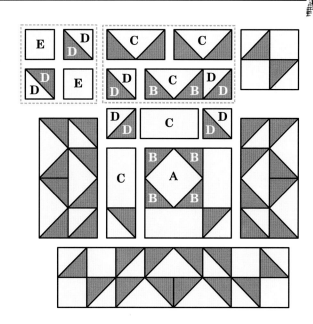

Piece	Fabric	Cut/Yield		Quick Cut
A	Light	1		3-1/2" square
B	Dark	28		2" sq. Connector Corner
C	Light	16		2 x 3-1/2" rectangles
D	Light	10	20	2-3/8" sq. cut into half-square triangles
D	Dark	10	20	2-3/8" sq. cut into half-square triangles
E	Light	8		2" squares

Assemble block following piecing diagram above. See helpful piecing instructions in Construction Tips & Advice. Connector Corners are used to simplify construction.

Lucretia's Lament
*By Peggy McKinney of
Greenwood, Indiana
54" x 54"*

"Those who go forth ministering to the wants and necessities of their fellow beings experience a rich return, their souls being as a watered garden and as a spring that faileth not."
Lucretia Mott

31

Sojourner Truth

**1797-1883
Antislavery
Activist**

"It is not easy to be a pioneer - but oh, it is fascinating! I would not trade one moment: even the worst moment, for all the riches in the world."
Elizabeth Blackwell

Isabella was born about 1797, the ninth child of James & Betsey who were slaves on a farm in upstate New York. Isabella's father was very tall and straight as a young man and this gave him the name of "Baumfree", which is low-Dutch for tree. Her mother was lovingly called Mau-mau Bett. Isabella's mother was fearful that this child would be sold into slavery as had her other children. Though the family was forced to live in crowded conditions with other slaves and work endlessly, Mau-mau Bett found the time to instill a deep abiding love of God in Isabella and her brother Peter. They were told that there was a God who lived in the sky who would always watch over them. They were taught to kneel and say the Lord's prayer whenever they would fall into trouble or were beaten. She encouraged them to never lie or steal and to obey their mas-

ters at all times. These humble instructions were treasured and held sacred by Isabella throughout her life.

Isabella and Thomas were married in 1814 and had five children over the next 12 years. While raising the children Isabella carried on the tradition of teaching them to never lie, never steal and always obey their master. Isabella was one of the first black women to win a lawsuit, when she sued to rescue her son Peter from slavery. In 1843 Isabella finally gained her freedom and over the next few years she worked as a servant in hopes of earning enough money to bring her family together.

In 1843 Isabella set out saying that, *"The Spirit calls me and I must go."* With little except her faith she said, *"Farewell, friends. I must be about my Father's business."* Feeling the need for a new name, Isabella prayed and the Lord gave her *"Sojourner because she was to travel up and down the land showing people their sins and being a sign unto them."* Later the Lord gave her Truth because she was sent to *"declare the truth unto the people."* Sojourner Truth's journey began.

Over the next few years Sojourner captivated audiences with her powerful speaking voice and strong powerful build. She could electrify listeners and became a regular speaker at community events. In the late 1840's a book about her travels was written by Oliver Gilbert called the *"**Narrative of Sojourner Truth**"*. She would travel from town to town and sell her book to raise money for her different causes. She quickly sold the entire first printing and even though her life was threatened, she would not stop her work. She stated that, *"I think of the great things of God, not the little things."* For 30 years she traveled

Sojourner Truth

around the country and spoke in twenty states for women's rights and the antislavery movement. In her travels through the Midwest she was often heckled by pro-slavery groups, but relied on her quick wit to quiet the critics. At one meeting a man told her, *"Old woman, I don't care any more for your talk than I do for the bite of a flea."* *"The Lord willing,"* she replied, *"I'll keep you scratching."*

In 1860, Truth returned home to recuperate from the rigors of her travels and was joined by her family, which gave her great comfort and reminded her that all her children had been released from slavery. When Abraham Lincoln signed the Emancipation Proclamation declaring all slaves in the Confederate states would be free on January 1, 1863, her energy was restored and she longed to begin work again. Friends arranged for the publication of a revised edition of ***The Narrative of Sojourner Truth***. With Harriet Beecher Stowe writing about their meeting, Truth's fame increased. Sojourner wished she were younger and stronger to continue the work for her cause.

During the Civil War, Truth traveled through camps bringing food and speaking about patriotism. She served food and sang hymns to help lift the spirits of the soldiers. Her ***Book of Life*** was her constant companion. As she took to the road to speak out for her chosen causes the empty pages of her ***Book of Life*** were signed by many important people. When she met with President Lincoln in 1864, she told him, *"I never heard of you before you were put in for president."* Lincoln laughed and replied, *"I heard of you years and years before I ever thought of being president."* Lincoln thanked her and signed her ***Book of Life***, *"For Aunty Sojourner Truth, A. Lincoln, Oct 29, 1864."* Although shattered by Lincoln's assassination, Truth was happy that she had lived to see the end of the war and of slavery when, on December 12, 1865, Congress ratified the Thirteenth Amendment to the U.S. Constitution.

On November 26, 1883, Sojourner Truth died in Battle Creek, Michigan. Many newspapers wrote, *"One of the greater Americans of our time has passed away but her passing will never silence her voice."* Thousands of mourners paid their respects, and as the sun was setting, Truth was sent to her final resting place.

Sojourner's friend, Oliver Gilbert, said *"... the sun lit up the skies and it seemed that it was unwilling to leave the earth in gloom."* Sojourner left a deep and inspiring legacy to anyone who faces a struggle in their life. We should remember one of her favorite lines;

"I want to tell you these things that you will always remember when I step out of this existence, you will know what old Sojourner told you. And Truth shall be my abiding name."

"Hear my prayer, O Lord, and give ear unto my cry; Hold not thy peace at my tears; for I am a stranger with thee, and sojourner as all my fathers were."
Psalms 39:12

33

Ain't I A Woman
By Kaye England
Quilted by Cathy Franks
33" x 50"

'That man... says that women need to be helped into carriages, and lifted over ditches, and to have the best place everywhere. Nobody ever helps me into carriages, over mud puddles, or gives me any best place, and ain't I a woman? ...I have plowed and planted and gathered into barns, and no man could head me - and ain't I a woman? I could work as much and eat as much as a man (when I could get it), and bear the lash as well and ain't I a woman? I have borne thirteen children and seen them most all sold off into slavery, and when I cried out with a mother's grief: none but Jesus heard - and ain't I a woman?"
Sojourner Truth
Ain't I A Woman speech, 1865

Sojourner Truth

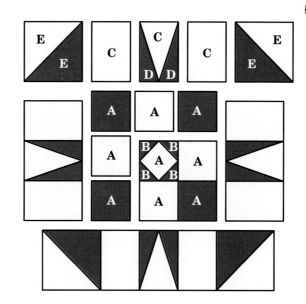

**Sojourner Truth
(12" Block)**

Piece	Fabric	Cut/Yield		Quick Cut
A	Light	5		2-1/2" square
A	Dark	4		2-1/2" squares
B	Dark	4		1-1/2" square Connector Corners
C	Light	12		2-1/2 x 3-1/2" rectangles
D	Dark	8		2-1/2 x 3-1/2" rectangle Connectors
E	Light	2	4	3-7/8" sq. cut into half-square triangles
E	Dark	2	4	3-7/8" sq. cut into half-square triangles

Assemble block following piecing diagram above. See helpful piecing instructions in Construction Tips & Advice. Connector Corners are used to simplify construction of this block.

Sojourner Truth and Abraham Lincoln.

"I am glad to see that men are getting their rights, but I want women to get theirs, and while the water is stirring I will step into the pool."
Sojourner Truth

Glory in Tribulation

Fabric Requirements

Background	1-1/4 yards
White print	1/4 yard
Dark green	1/4 yard
Dark purple	1/4 yard
Dark print	1-1/3 yards
Backing	1-1/4 yards

Center Blocks

Make five Sojourner Truth blocks following piecing diagram on page 35, see photo below for color placement.

Set On-Point

Cut a 19" square of the Dark print and crosscut into quarter-square setting triangles. Cut four 3-1/2" square Connector Corners from Background fabric and sew onto the setting triangles as illustrated. Following photo, set blocks in on-point setting using quarter-square triangles to fill in sides.

Cut an 11" square of Dark print and cut diagonally into half-square triangles. Sew these to corners to "square" off the quilt.

Square quilt to 34-1/2" square.

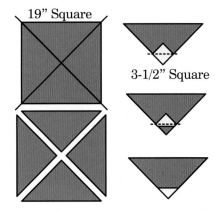

Connector Corner on Setting Triangles

Border One

Cut the following:

Dark print	2	1-1/2 x 34-1/2" strips
Dark print	2	1-1/2 x 36-1/2" strips

Join shorter strips to sides and longer ones to opposite top and bottom.

Border Two

Using Dark green print and background fabric, cut from each 26 3-7/8" squares cut into half-squares triangles. Sew into squares. (Speed this up by gridding your triangles or using one of the great triangle papers).

Sew into strips as in photo and sew shorter strips to sides, and longer ones to top and bottom.

Finishing

Quilt, bind and enjoy!

Glory in Tribulation
By Laurie Keller of Indianapolis, Indiana
42" x 42"

Glory in Tribulation

The Valiant Soldiers

We are the valiant soldiers who've 'listed for the war;
We are fighting for the Union, we are fighting for the law;
We can shoot a rebel farther than a white man ever saw;
As we go marching on.

Chorus: Glory, glory hallelujah! Glory, glory hallelujah!
Glory, glory hallelujah, as we go marching on.

Look there above the center, where the flag is waving bright:
We are going out of slavery, we are bound for freedom's light;
We mean to show Jeff Davis how the Africans can fight:
As we go marching on. — Chorus

We are done with hoeing cotton, we are done with hoeing corn:
We are colored Yankee soldiers as sure as you are born.
When massa hears us shouting, he will think 'tis Gabriel's horn,
As we go marching on — Chorus

They will have to pay us wages, the wages of their sin:
They will have to bow their foreheads to their colored kith and kin:
They will have to give us house-room, or the roof will tumble in,
As we go marching on — Chorus

We hear the proclamation, massa, hush it as you will;
The birds will sing it to us, hopping on the cotton hill:
The possum up the gum tree couldn't keep it still,
As he went climbing on — Chorus

Father Abraham has spoken, and the message has been sent:
The prison doors have opened, and out the prisoners went
To join the sable army of African descent,
As we go marching on — Chorus
Sojourner Truth
Sing to the tune of "John Brown's Body"
(Battle Hymn of the Republic)

Julia Ward Howe

**1819 - 1910
Author,
Social
Reformer**

"The very intensity of our feeling for home, husband and children gives us a power of loving and working outside our homes, to redeem the world as love and work only can."
Julia Ward Howe

Julia Ward was born in New York City, May 27, 1819 to Samuel and Julia Cuttle Ward. Her father was a banker and gave Julia every advantage of a liberal education. She was taught at home by capable teachers in Greek, German, French, music and was a bright and earnest student. She read ***Pilgrim's Progress*** when she was nine, was writing religious verse by the time she was twelve and became a lifelong student of German literature and philosophy.

In 1843 she married Dr. Samuel Howe and moved to Boston, where he headed the Perkins Institution for the Blind. Since Dr. Howe did not believe in women's involvement in public life, Julia spent the next two decades rearing their six children, reading and writing. She developed the method for teaching language to a blind deaf mute. She won the gratitude of Greece when she extended aid in their struggle for independence. During these years she also penned verses and published her first volume, ***Passion Flowers***, in 1854. She and her husband also published the ***Commonwealth***, an abolitionist newspaper.

In the fall of 1861 while they were in Washington, D.C., Union troops marched by their carriage singing "John Brown's Body." It was suggested that she pen new words to this popular old tune. In the morning she described the following events;

"I awoke... in the gray of the early dawn, and to my astonishment found that the wished-for lines were arranging themselves in my brain. I lay quite still until the last verse had completed itself in my thoughts, then hastily arose, saying to myself; I shall lose this if I don't write it down immediately."

The Atlantic Monthly first published the poem in February 1862 and the "Battle Hymn of the Republic" became the most popular song for the North. The editor, James T. Fields, paid her $5 for the piece and is credited with having given the title to the lyrics. This new found notoriety opened many doors for her, and she quickly entered a public life which centered her interests on women's causes.

After the war, she helped found the New England Woman Suffrage Association, the American Women Suffrage Association, served as president of the associations in New England and Massachusetts and for years edited the ***Women's Journal***. She was a very effective speaker and lectured extensively throughout the country over the next few years. Julia was a staunch supporter for the causes of women and peace and in 1870, published her "***Appeal to Womanhood Throughout the World***," a call for an international conference of women on the subject of peace. She was adored

Julia Ward Howe

by a nation and was known as the "Dearest Old Lady in America." Julia published many poems and articles during her life, and was the first woman elected to the American Academy of Arts and Letters.

On October 17, 1910 Julia Ward Howe died of pneumonia in Portsmouth, Rhode Island, at her home on Union Street where Howe had said, *"My days have been precious."* At her funeral over 4000 mourners sang the *Battle Hymn of the Republic.* She was laid to rest in Mount Auburn Cemetery, next to her husband, the man who at first would not allow her to work outside the home. She had summarized their difficult marriage by saying, *"I have never known my husband to approve of any act of mine which I myself valued."* After his death in 1876 Julia had thirty-four years to devote to her interests.

Julia Ward Howe left many legacies, but certainly the one most well known would be the soulful words to the Battle Hymn of the Republic. These lyrics immediately stir our innermost emotions and we remember.

Mine Eyes Have Seen the Glory
*By Kaye England & Friends
Quilted by
Leona Berg
46" x 50"*

"When God thought of Mother, he must have laughed with satisfaction, and framed it quickly – so rich, so deep, so divine, so full of soul, power, and beauty, was the conception."
Henry Ward Beecher

39

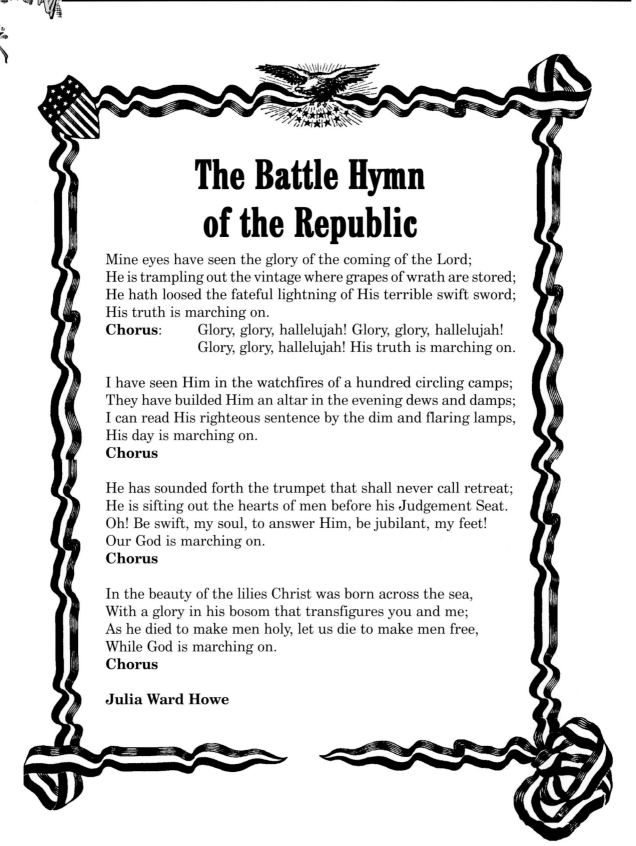

The Battle Hymn of the Republic

Mine eyes have seen the glory of the coming of the Lord;
He is trampling out the vintage where grapes of wrath are stored;
He hath loosed the fateful lightning of His terrible swift sword;
His truth is marching on.

Chorus: Glory, glory, hallelujah! Glory, glory, hallelujah!
Glory, glory, hallelujah! His truth is marching on.

I have seen Him in the watchfires of a hundred circling camps;
They have builded Him an altar in the evening dews and damps;
I can read His righteous sentence by the dim and flaring lamps,
His day is marching on.
Chorus

He has sounded forth the trumpet that shall never call retreat;
He is sifting out the hearts of men before his Judgement Seat.
Oh! Be swift, my soul, to answer Him, be jubilant, my feet!
Our God is marching on.
Chorus

In the beauty of the lilies Christ was born across the sea,
With a glory in his bosom that transfigures you and me;
As he died to make men holy, let us die to make men free,
While God is marching on.
Chorus

Julia Ward Howe

Julia Ward Howe

Julia Ward Howe
(12" Block)

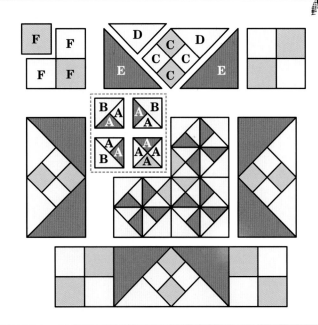

Assemble block following piecing diagram above.

Piece	Fabric	Cut	/Yield	Quick Cut
A	Light	5	20	2-3/4" sq. cut into quarter-square triangles
A	Dark	4	16	2-3/4" sq. cut into quarter-square triangles
A	Medium	1	4	2-3/4" sq. cut into quarter-square triangles
B	Light	6	12	2-3/8" sq. cut into half-square triangles
C	Light	8		1-1/2" squares
C	Medium	8		1-1/2" squares
D	Light	2	8	4-1/4" sq. cut into quarter-square triangles
E	Dark	4	8	3-7/8" sq. cut into half-square triangles
F	Light	8		2" squares
F	Medium	8		2" squares

Glory, Glory, Hallelujah!
By Alice Cunningham of
Carmel, Indiana
38" x 38"

"Clouds and darkness surround us, yet Heaven is just, and the day of triumph will surely come, when justice and truth will be vindicated. Our wrongs will be made right, and we will once more, taste the blessings of freedom."
Mary Todd Lincoln

Harriet Beecher Stowe

"Many a humble soul will be amazed to find that the seed it sowed in weakness, in the dust of daily life, has blossomed into immortal flowers under the eye of the Lord."
Harriet Beecher Stowe

arriet Elizabeth Beecher was born on June 14, 1811 in Litchfield, Connecticut to parents Lyman and Roxana Foote Beecher who lived on an elm-shaded street with a house full of children, relatives and animals. The untimely passing of her mother put Harriet's rearing in the hands of her aunts, older sister and later on a stepmother. During this time her father, the Reverend Lyman Beecher, was a tremendous influence on her life and was fast becoming one of the century's most popular preachers.

Harriet received five years of schooling in Litchfield and three years at her sister Catherine's school in Hartford where she later taught for five years. In 1832 when the family moved to Cincinnati, Harriet again taught for her sister Catherine at the Western Female Institute. In 1833 while on a visit to a Kentucky plantation Harriet glimpsed slavery in ac-

tion. She committed all of these going-ons to memory before returning home.

She soon became friends with Professor Calvin Stowe and his wife Eliza while sharing interests and attending many meetings together. A short year later Eliza Stowe died from cholera when an epidemic swept the city in 1834. Both husband and friend were shattered but their friendship saw them through the dark days. Slowly they fell in love and on January 6, 1836 were married. Harriet supplemented their income by writing stories and sketches for periodicals. The birth of four children kept Harriet in poor health for years while her household duties seemed never ending. By 1848 their household had grown to six children and in the summer of 1849 a horrific cholera epidemic hit Cincinnati striking their son Samuel Charles. Calvin was away leaving Harriet alone to watch their small child loose his battle. Stowe wrote to her husband;

"At last it is over and our dear little one is gone from us. I write as though there were no sorrow like my sorrow yet there has been in this city, as in the land of Egypt, scarce a house without its dead."

When they moved to Maine in 1850, there was more money for the young family and another child was welcomed. At this time Harriet began writing a novel about slavery based on her readings of abolitionist literature and her personal observations. This tale was published in the **National Era** in 1851-1852 in forty episodes and was an immediate sensation. **Uncle Tom's Cabin** was strongly denounced through the south, but with sales of over 300,000 copies during the first year, an influence unequaled was placed in history.

Harriet Beecher Stowe

The book quickly became a strong influence on the nation's conscience and fanned the flames that would eventually erupt into the Civil War. The Stowe's lived only two years in the Brunswick, Maine house where **Uncle Tom's Cabin** was written before moving to Massachusetts in 1852. They remained there for twelve years during which time sadness again struck the family when their oldest son died in a drowning accident.

Although President Lincoln didn't at first espouse abolition as the reason for the war, Stowe viewed it as the North's crusade for emancipation. She was later to compose a speech attacking President Lincoln stating;

"My paramount object is to set at liberty them that are bruised and not either to save or destroy the Union. What I do in favor of the Union, I do because it helps to free the oppressed; what I forebear, I forebear because it does not help to free the oppressed."

Harriet Beecher Stowe
*By Caryl Schuetz of
Indianapolis, Indiana
35" x 50"*

Cabin Among the Stars
*By Kathy Saunders of
Cincinnati, Ohio
60" x 60"*

"When you get into a tight place and it seems you can't go on, hold on, for that's just the place and the time that the tide will turn. "
Harriet Beecher Stowe

43

Harriet Beecher Stowe

In November 1862 Stowe visited the president accompanied by her 26-year old daughter Harriet and 12-year old son Charles. She and Lincoln visited for about an hour and while she was impressed with President Lincoln's honesty, Lincoln said upon meeting Stowe, *"So this is the little lady who made this great war."* At a celebration marking the signing of the Emancipation Proclamation, Harriet was recognized and cheered by the crowd. Immensely honored she bowed and wiped away her tears. This honor would stay forever in her heart and the event would remain forever in the nation's memory. The country was still divided in war, blacks still lived in bondage and Harriet Beecher Stowe kept to her mission.

During the last year of the war Calvin Stowe retired while his wife continued the leadership of the family. They returned to Connecticut where Harriet's writings continued supporting her family. The assassination of Lincoln and the end of a terrible war were events that stirred strong emotions in Stowe. This horrible war had cost the country over 600,000 young men but Congress had enacted the Thirteenth Amendment to the Constitution that would forever outlaw slavery.

Harriet and Calvin began spending winters in Florida but due to deteriorating health, they returned to Connecticut and welcomed their quiet hours spent together. Calvin Stowe became ill and on August 6, 1886 passed away with his wife by his side. This loss was devastating to Harriet, but she continued on writing the *"**Life of Harriet Beecher Stowe**"* with the aid of her youngest son. She spent her days working in the garden, writing letters and remembering times gone by.

She died at Hartford, Connecticut on July 1, 1896 and was buried in Andover, Massachusetts beside her husband in the family plot. Friends and family gathered by her graveside to sing a hymn that Stowe had composed, reflecting her thoughts about death and God:

"It lies around us like a cloud, A world we do not see, Yet the sweet closing of an eye, may bring us there to be."

I designed the block with a star center for the star that guided many slaves to freedom, an alternate center features a log cabin. An entire nation marveled at her strength and perseverance while as women we are honored remembering her quote; *"Women are the real architects of society. "*

Harriet Beecher Stowe
By Carol Grimstad of
Indianapolis, Indiana
44" x 44"

Harriet Beecher Stowe

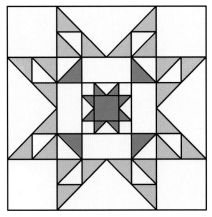

**Harriet Beecher Stowe
(12" Block)**

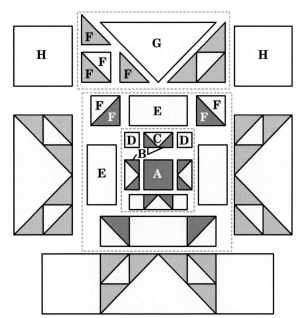

Piece Fabric Cut/Yield Cutting Instructions

Center Star

Piece	Fabric	Cut	Yield	Cutting Instructions
A	Medium	1		2" square
B	Dark	8		1-1/4" square Connector Corners
C	Light	4		1-1/4 x 2" rectangles
D	Light	4		1-1/4" squares
E	Light	4		2 x 3-1/2" rectangles
F	Light	2	4	2-3/8" sq. cut into half-square triangles
F	Dark	2	4	2-3/8" sq. cut into half-square triangles

Outside Star

Piece	Fabric	Cut	Yield	Cutting Instructions
G	Light	1	4	7-1/4" sq. cut into quarter-square triangles
F	Light	4	8	2-3/8" sq. cut into half-square triangles
F	Medium	12	24	2-3/8" sq. cut into half-square triangles
H	Light	4		3-1/2" squares

Center Log Cabin

Piece	Fabric	Cut	Cutting Instructions
J	Ground	1	2 x 6-1/2" rectangle
K	Side	2	1-1/2 x 2" rectangle
K	Front	2	1-1/2 x 2" rectangle
K	Door	1	1-1/2 x 2" rectangle
K	Sky	1	1-1/2 x 2" rectangle
L	Window	1	1-1/2 x 1-1/4" rectangle
L	Side	1	1-1/2 x 1-1/4" rectangle
L	Sky	2	1-1/2 x 1-1/4" rectangle
L	Chimney	2	1-1/2 x 1-1/4" rectangle
M	Sky	2	2" square Connector Corner
M	Roof	1	2" square Connector Corner
N	Peak	1	2 x 3-1/2" rectangle
N	Roof	1	2 x 3-1/2" rectangle
P	Sky	2	2" squares

"I have been the mother of seven children, the most beautiful and most loved whom lies buried near my Cincinnati residence. It was at his dying bed and at his grave that I learned what a poor slave mother may feel when her child is torn away from her. In those depths of sorrow which seemed to me immeasurable, it was my only prayer to God that such anguish might not be suffered in vain. There were circumstances about his death of such peculiar bitterness, of what seemed almost cruel suffering that I felt I could never be consoled for it, unless this crushing of my own heart might enable me to work out some great good to others.

I allude to this here because I have often felt that much that is in that book had its root in the awful scenes and bitter sorrow of that summer. It has left now I trust no trace on my mind except a deep compassion for the sorrowful, especially for mothers who are separated from their children."

Harriet Beecher Stowe

Assemble block following drawing above. See helpful piecing instructions in Construction Tips & Advice.

45

Fabric Requirements

Black (cabins, borders)	3/4 yard
Assorted Teals (geese)	1/3 yard
Assorted Reds (border)	1/2 yard
Gold (center cabin star)	1/4 yard
Dark Backgmd (border)	1/2 yard
Light Background	1/2 yard
Floral (border)	1 yard
Assorted Browns	scraps
Backing and Binding	3 yards

Log Cabins

Follow assembly diagram below, make five Log Cabin centers, set four aside for later use. Complete the star diagrammed on previous page, using light background and gold fabrics.

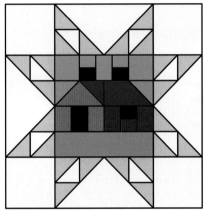

Alternate Center for Harriet Beecher Stowe Block (12" Block)

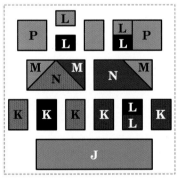

Border One

Cut the following:
Black fabric 2 1-1/2 x 12-1/2" strips
Black fabric 2 1-1/2 x 14-1/2" strips
Attach short strips to sides and longer ones to top and bottom.

Border Two (Flying Geese)

Cut forty 2-1/4 x 4" rectangles for the base of the Flying Geese, add a 2-1/4" Connector Corner square to each end (see diagram). Join these into strips of eight, attach two of these to sides. To the remaining two strips add two Flying Geese to one end (pointing in the same direction as the side border they attach to). Join these to top and bottom.

Border Three

Cut the following:
Black fabric 2 2 x 21-1/2" strips
Black fabric 2 2 x 24-1/2" strips
Attach short strips to sides and longer ones to top and bottom.

Border Four (Large Star)

Follow illustration below to make eight large units and four small units using assorted reds and dark background fabrics. For sides join two large units into a strip and attach. For top and bottom join two large units and two small units (see diagram) and attach.

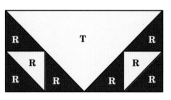

Border Four

Piece	Fabric	Cut	Yield	Cutting Instructions
R	Bkgrds	10	20	3-7/8" sq. cut into half-sq. triangles
R	Reds	30	60	3-7/8" sq. cut into half-sq. triangles
S	Bkgrds	2	4	6-7/8" sq. cut into half-sq. triangles
T	Bkgrds	4	8	13-1/4" sq. cut into quarter-sq. tri's

Harriet Beecher Stowe

Border Five
Cut the following:
Black fabric   2   1-1/2 x 36-1/2" strips
Black fabric   2   1-1/2 x 38-1/2" strips
Attach short strips to sides and longer ones to top and bottom.

Border Six (Cabins)
Cut the following:
Floral fabric   4   6-1/2 x 36-1/2" strips
Black fabric   8   1-1/2 x 6-1/2" strips
Attach a black strip to each end of floral strips. Attach to sides. Add a Cabin center to each end of remaining two strips (make sure they face the proper direction) and attach to top and bottom.

Border Seven
For the last time cut the following :
Black fabric   2   1-1/2 x 50-1/2" strips
Black fabric   2   1-1/2 x 52-1/2" strips

Finishing
Square up the quilt top, sandwich with batting and backing, quilt using your favorite hand or machine technique, and bind.

Harriet Beecher Stowe
By Marianne Roan of Indianapolis, Indiana 52" x 52"

"If I could I would always work in silence and obscurity, and let my efforts be known by their results."
Emily Bronte

Louisa May Alcott

**1832-1888
Author**

Louisa May Alcott was born in Germantown, Pennsylvania on November 29, 1832, sharing a birthday with her father, Amos Bronson Alcott, an educator and philosopher. Most of her life was grounded in the Boston area where at an early age she was friends with the likes of Ralph Waldo Emerson and Henry David Thoreau. Most of her education was at her father's Temple School in Boston and later at home. He was a stern moralist who prescribed reading **Pilgrim's Progress** and partaking of a meatless diet. Wife Abigail was the anchor of the family and very close to Louisa. After Bronson's Temple School failed, the family moved to Concord in 1840 where Louisa wrote her first poem.

Bronson Alcott's failures had a deep affect on Louisa, and at thirteen she would write in her journal the resolve to "teach, sew, act, write, or any-thing to help the family." Louisa wrote plays she and her sisters staged for their company at a moment's notice.

Her first published story appeared in the *Saturday Evening Gazette* in 1854 under another author's name and later was followed by a group of fairy stories penned under her own name. During her life she worked as a seamstress, teacher and domestic to supplement her income from writing. During the Civil War she served as an Army nurse in Washington suffering a near-fatal illness that affected her remaining years. She wrote of these experiences in "*Hospital Sketches*" which appeared in serial form.

Louisa worked as editor for a girl's magazine in 1867. At the urging of her publisher friend Thomas Niles she began work on a book that would become her greatest achievement. She moved from Boston to her family home in Concord to write the first volume which was published in September 1868 and finished the second volume in January 1869. **Little Women** was an autobiographical depiction of the warmth and love of a family in the middle-class North during the Civil War. The "girls" were quickly recognized: Louisa as the long suffering Jo; Anna as the story's romantic Meg; gentle Beth was the shy sweet Beth of the story and May as the charming but annoying Amy. Her dear mother Abba was Marmee and Louisa's father Bronson was cast as the much loved but rarely seen Mr. March. Meg, Jo, Beth and Amy were an instant success as readers of all ages laughed and cried over the family's adventures and longed to know more about them. The success of **Little Women** would change life for the Alcotts as they could now pay their bills and splurge on luxuries.

"Love is the only thing that we can carry with us when we go, and it makes the end so easy."
Louisa May Alcott

48

Louisa May Alcott

Louisa spent many years summering in Concord but wrote mostly in Boston during the winters. She was interested in the suffrage movement and when she was accused of being against the movement, stated: *"I should be a traitor to all I most love, if I did not covet a place among those who are giving their lives to the emancipation of the white slaves of America."* She participated in charitable works, sharing stories with the prisoners at Concord State Reformatory and entertaining the poor and infirm with storytelling. She was also active in abolition, temperance, suffrage and labor throughout her life.

Although Louisa had achieved fame, her personal life brought her little joy. She was dominated by her family and sense of duty all her life, spending both her youth and adulthood caring for others. Throughout her last twenty years, but for a brief tour of Europe in 1870, Louisa lived in Boston and Concord caring for her mother who died after a long illness in 1877 and later caring for her helpless father. She had shielded him from his friends and admirers while marveling at his beautiful serenity. Saddened by his condition, Louisa wrote, *"These painless, peaceful days have a certain sweetness."* She later adopted the children of two of her sisters who had died prematurely.

Louisa May Alcott
By Cindy Sochar of Westfield, Indiana Quilted by Cecelia A. Purciful
60" x 60"

"Love is a great beautifier."
Louisa May Alcott

Louisa May Alcott

The strain of caring for her father and the children took its toll on Louisa and she died at Boston just two days after her father on March 6, 1888. She lay in a coma never knowing that Bronson Alcott had gone before her. Louisa had learned from **Pilgrim's Progress** to "*Bear your burdens gladly,*" and she had borne hers well. She had written,

"*Oh, when these hidden stores of ours lie open to the Father's sight may they be rich in golden hours, Deeds that show fairer for the light, Lives whose brave music long shall ring with a spirit-stirring strain, Souls that shall gladly soar and sing In the long sunlight after rain.*"

Louisa was laid to rest on author's ridge at Concord, Massachusetts in Sleepy Hollow Cemetery, surrounded by the likes of Emerson, Thoreau and Hawthorne. Having never married, Louisa had said that, "*...my books are my children and the pen is my husband.*"

As generations of young women continue to enjoy and learn from the writings of Louisa May Alcott, I designed a block for her with a star in each of the corners to represent the "*girls*", Jo, Meg, Amy and Beth, and the center star for dear mother Marmee. Louisa May Alcott's home in Concord now serves as a Memorial Association and the house is filled with remembrances of this unique family. As Thoreau wrote;

"*If one advances confidently in the direction of his dreams, and endeavors to live the life which he has imagined, he will meet a success unexpected in common hours.*"

Perhaps he was thinking of Louisa May Alcott!

Little Women
By Mary Beth Haas of Edmond, Oklahoma 38" x 38"

"*You have a good many little gifts and virtues, but there is no need of parading them, for conceit spoils the finest genius. There is not much danger that real talent or goodness will be overlooked long, and the great charm of all power is modesty.*"
Louisa May Alcott

Louisa May Alcott

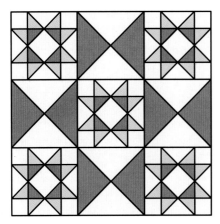

**Louisa May Alcott
(12" Block)**

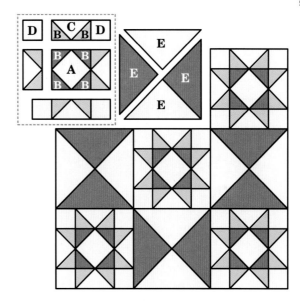

Piece	Fabric	Cut	Yield	Cutting Instructions
A	Light	5		2-1/2" squares
B	Dark	20		1-1/2" square Connector Corners
B	Medium	40		1-1/2" square Connector Corners
C	Light	20		1-1/2 x 2-1/2" rectangles
D	Light	20		1-1/2" squares
E	Light	2	8	5-1/4" sq. cut into quarter-square triangles
E	Dark	2	8	5-1/4" sq. cut into quarter-square triangles

Assemble block following drawing above. See helpful piecing instructions in Construction Tips & Advice.

Stars Over Orchard House
*By Melissa Taylor of
Greenwood, Indiana
48" x 48"*

"I am not afraid of storms for I am learning how to sail my ship."
Louisa May Alcott

Helen Adams Keller

**1880-1968
Author,
Lecturer and
Humanitarian**

*"Keep your face to
the sunshine and
you cannot see the
shadows."*
Helen Keller

Helen Adams Keller was born on June 27, 1880, near Tuscumbia, Alabama. At the young and innocent age of 19 months she was stricken with a raging fever which left her blind and deaf. Helen was sentenced to a silent and lonely place most could not comprehend until she was examined by a family friend, Alexander Graham Bell, at the age of six. Anne Sullivan was sent from the Perkins Institution to work with Helen and within months had calmed her wild behavior, opening a world of unparalleled achievement. Through this constant and patient guidance, Helen learned to read, write, speak and graduated cum laude from Radcliffe College in 1904. Helen Keller's courage, faith and perspective became known worldwide touching many people and her accomplishments should forever stand as a symbol of human potential.

Studying Helen Keller's life, I became aware of this dazzling mind and how she touched so many people. Helen was fond of all living things and developed a tendency to modify the facts and to block out the violent, disgusting and the distasteful. It has been written that, *"Her mind is as clear as her brain is fertile, while her heart flames with earnestness and glows with charity."* *"Teacher"* as Helen referred to Anne Sullivan, spoke that;

"Helen 's mind was so gifted by nature that she was able to understand, with only the faintest touch of explanation, every possible variety of external relations. Our language seemed to paint on her memory indelible impressions and her language would begin with wonderful accuracy, like the reflection from a mirror."

When Helen was asked by a reporter how she could be so happy, she stated;

"I have lost only two of God's gifts and still have many powers, the greatest of all is a mind that can be cultivated, and through which I can enjoy most of God's blessings."

Alexander Bell stated, *"I feel that in this child I have seen more of the Divine than has been manifest in anyone I ever met before."*

Her constant companion Anne Sullivan married John Macy, with the understanding that Helen would be her permanent charge. It seemed that theirs was such a magical friendship even the bonds of marriage could not intervene, so Anne and John were divorced. Polly Thompson then came into Helen's life and would remain a lifelong companion and helper.

Helen authored several articles, books and biographies, was active on the staff of the Foundation for the Blind and lectured in over twenty-five

Helen Adams Keller

countries, receiving many awards. She became actively involved in the women's suffrage movement and causes of the blind. As her world continued to fill, she became a legend, making a movie, participating in peace rallies and fund raising for the American Foundation for the Blind. Helen was a regular visitor of military hospitals during World War II and a source of consolation for injured veterans. Many people who had been touched by Helen's life stated that along with the overpowering level of intelligence and rare sensitivity, was the overwhelming sense of joy Helen possessed that endeared her so.

Helen's beloved "Teacher" passed away on October 20, 1936. At the committal service of the ashes, Helen spoke; *"Blessings upon the receptacle of the precious dust which my heaven-sent Teacher wore as a garment as she wrought her miracle of liberation through Him who is the Lord of Life and Love."* Helen, with the support of Polly, continued in her travels and teachings.

Polly Thompson died on March 21, 1960 and Helen wrote:

"Now I sit by her empty chair thinking of the fidelity with which she helped me in my difficult work and the tireless cheer with which she took part in our amazing adventures. I am sure that now they have met in Heaven, Teacher is prouder of Polly than ever. It will be most lonely for me, but I shall rejoice in Polly's beautiful new life."

Helen Keller died June 1, 1968, at Westport, Connecticut and her ashes were placed in the columbarium at the National Cathedral in Washington, alongside her beloved Teacher and Polly. In the closing tribute to Helen Keller, a quotation from ***My Rebellion*** was read;

"What is so sweet as to awake from a troubled dream and behold a beloved face smiling upon you? I have to believe that such shall be our awakening from earth to heaven. My faith never wavers that each dear friend I have "lost" is a new link between this world and the happier land beyond the morn. My soul is for the moment bowed down with grief when I cease to feel the touch of their hands or hear a tender word from them; but the light of faith never fades from my sky."

In the company of many Presidents, world figures, and movie stars, Helen Keller was also at ease with the average person giving of herself generously. She never failed to give credit for her accomplishments to her family and friends that gave of their life that she may conquer. Helen was awarded the Presidential Medal of Freedom and was universally acknowledged as one of the greatest women in the world. Volumes have been written about this uncommon woman, yet she best summed up her own being with this simple quote:

"It gives me a deep comforting sense that all things seen are temporal, and things unseen are eternal. "

Helen Keller loved flowers and was photographed on many occasions with roses. I designed this block with flowers in each corner to represent the roses she loved and the star in the center representing the illuminated force that Helen Keller brought to all mankind. Could anyone know of her accomplishments and not be somehow encouraged that life can be worthy, serviceable and fulfilling if only we reach into the depths of our soul?

"Avoiding danger is no safer in the long run than outright exposure. The fearful are caught as often as the bold."
Helen Keller

Helen Adams Keller

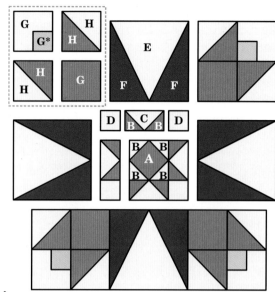

Helen Keller
(12" Block)

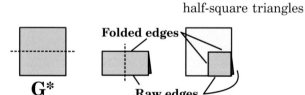

Piece Fabric Cut/Yield Cutting Instructions

Piece	Fabric	Cut/Yield		Cutting Instructions
A	Medium	1		2-1/2" square
B	Light	4		1-1/2" square Connector Corners
B	Medium	8		1-1/2" square Connector Corners
C	Light	4		1-1/2 x 2-1/2" rectangles
D	Light	4		1-1/2" squares
E	Light	4		4-1/2" squares
F	Dark	8		4-1/2" square Bias Connectors
G	Medium	4		2-1/2" squares
G	Light	4		2-1/2" squares
G*	Rosebud	4		2-1/2" square
H	Light	4	8	2-7/8" sq. cut into half-square triangles
H	Medium	4	8	2-7/8" sq. cut into half-square triangles

Assemble block following piecing diagram above. See helpful piecing instructions in Construction Tips & Advice. Quick piecing techniques are used to simplify construction.

Folded edges

Raw edges

G*

*For rosebud "G", fold fabric in half, then again to form a square. Match raw edges to edges of background square, continue sewing. See diagram.

"Optimism is the faith that leads to achievement. Nothing can be done without hope and confidence."
Helen Keller

Helen Keller's Rose Garden
By Kaye England
60 x 73"

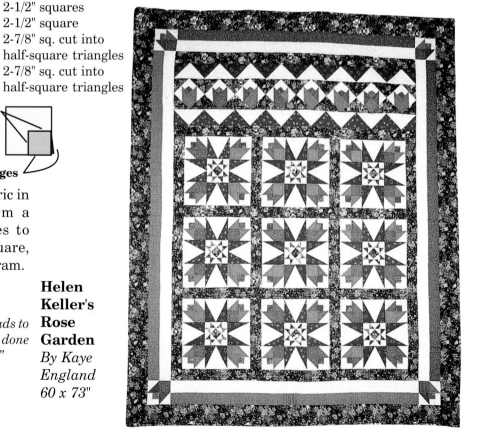

Helen Adams Keller

Fabric Requirements

Light background	2-1/4 yards
Purple print	1-1/2 yards
Green print	1-1/4 yards
Dark floral print	3 yards
Dark pink fabric	1/3 yard
Backing	3-2/3 yards

Center

Following piecing diagram on page 54, make nine Helen Keller blocks. Assemble into rows with sashing Cut the following

Dark floral	6	2-1/2 x 12-1/2" strips
Dark floral	2	2-1/2" x 40-1/2" strips

Following layout in photo make rows, then join with longer strips.

Border One

Cut the following:

Dark floral	2	2-1/2 x 40-1/2" strips
Dark floral	2	2-1/2 x 44-1/2" strips

Attach shorter strips to sides and longer ones to top and bottom.

Rose Border Row One

Make eight Flying Geese. Cut the following:

Light bkgrd	8	3-1/4 x 6" rectangles
Dark floral	16	3-1/4" sq. Connectors

Add a Connector to each end of rectangles, sew diagonally through each, trim Connector to 1/4", fold and press down (see diagram). Join into a strip.

Rose Border Row Two

See illustration below and make eight flower units and frame as follows:
Cut the following:

Dark floral	16	3-5/8" sq, cut diag.

Attach four of these to each flower unit to make a square. Join these into a strip.

Rose Border Row Three

Repeat Rose Border Row One.

Rose Border Row Four

From Dark floral print cut a 2-1/2 x 44-1/2" strip.
Join the four rows as shown and attach to quilt top.

Outer Border One

Cut the following:

Background	2	2-1/2 x 44-1/2" strips
Background	2	2-1/2 x 57-1/2" strips
Green print	2	2-1/2 x 44-1/2" strips
Green print	2	2-1/2 x 57-1/2" strips

Sew short Light strips to short Green strips and attach to sides.
Make four more flower units.
Sew long Light strips to long Green strips, add a flower unit to ends, then attach to top and bottom of quilt.

Outer Border Two

Cut the following:

Dark floral	2	4-1/2 x 68-1/2" strips
Dark floral	2	4-1/2 x 64-1/2" strips

Attach shorter strips to sides and longer strips to top and bottom.

Finish

Quilt and bind your completed top with your favorite technique.

They took away what should have been my eyes,
(But I remembered Milton's Paradise.)
They took away what should have been my ears,
(Beethoven came and wiped away my tears.)
They took away what should have been my tongue,
(But I had talked with God when I was young.)
He would not let them take away my soul,
Possessing that, I still possess the whole.
Helen Keller

Sarah Breedlove "Madam C.J." Walker

1867 - 1919
Businesswoman

"*If the future road looks ominous or unpromising, and the roads back vanishing then we need to gather our resolve and, carrying only the necessary baggage, step off that road into another direction.*"
Maya Angelou

56

Sarah Breedlove was born December 23, 1867, the daughter of poor farmers on a cotton plantation in Delta, Louisiana. She was the first member of her family to be born free and her parents Owen and Minerva Breedlove held high hopes that their daughter's life would be different than their own. The first Christmas of Sarah's life followed bad crops and without presents for her brother and sister, Alex and Louvenia, Sarah became the family's very special gift. Though the Breedlove's were free, they had nowhere to go so they continued to work for their former owners as sharecroppers.

Sarah lost her parents in 1874, at the young age of seven leaving her very isolated and frightened. Over the next few years, Sarah and Louvenia supported themselves in Vicksburg, by taking in wash and serving other households. Sarah married at the age of 14, to escape a cruel brother-in-law and thought that Moses McWilliams would deliver her according to his biblical namesake. On June 6, 1885, at the age of 17, Sarah gave birth to a beautiful daughter, Lelia. In 1887, Moses died and once again Sarah was left alone, this time with a child to raise. She decided to leave for St. Louis in hopes of a better life for her and Lelia.

Sarah continued to take in wash, and years later she stated that;

"*As I bent over the washboard and looked at my arms buried in the soapsuds, I said to myself; 'What are you going to do when you grow old and your back gets stiff?' This set me to thinking, but without my thinking, I couldn't see how I, a poor washerwoman, was going to better my condition.*"

Sarah took pride in the fact that she could support her daughter by taking in laundry and was determined to complete her tasks to the best of her ability. By working hard, scrimping and saving, Sarah was able to send Lelia to college at Knoxville, Tennessee. During this time she began developing products for hair care and in time she arrived at a mixture that would ultimately make her famous.

Sarah continued developing her hair care line, taking in laundry, and selling her products door to door. Advertising in newspapers began generating mail orders and the business flourished. While in St. Louis, Sarah had become friends with Charles Joseph Walker, known as C.J, and he continued to advise her by mail. Eventually C.J. showed up in person, they fell in love and married on January 4, 1906. C.J. began promotions for his wife, handling all the advertisements and shortly thereafter Sarah began calling herself Madam C.J. Walker,

Sarah Breedlove "Madam C.J." Walker

believing that the title Madam made her seem more professional. By the time Lelia was 21 and graduated from college, she moved to Denver to help in the business. They added selling agents and increased their income beyond all expectations. Madam Walker moved her operations to Pittsburgh, and opened Lelia College, a beauty parlor and training school for her sales agents. The business continued to grow, but Sarah again wanted to move and selected Indianapolis for her new factory. After only one year in Indianapolis, she had approximately one-thousand agents selling her products throughout the country, and a decision was made to build a larger factory and office building. During this time Sarah and C.J. began to have differences, and although they divorced in 1912, she retained his name for the rest of her life.

Walker continued her tireless work spending the next years traveling and promoting her business. After her daughter had moved to New York, Sarah began to spend considerable time there, finally deciding to move but to leave her factory based in Indianapolis. After six years in Indianapolis, she had become the most famous businesswoman of her race. Her great success came from a strong self-confidence as she endeavored to benefit women of her race. Her advice was, *"Don't sit down and wait for opportunities to come... Get up and make them!"* By 1916 she employed over 20,000 agents and her earnings were in the six figures.

In 1917, Walker built a magnificent dream home in New York and named it the Villa Lewaro after her daughter. Madam Walker spent much of her time in philanthropies, including the NAACP, Tuskegee Institute and various Indianapolis institutions.

She was very involved in community work encouraging many black women to improve their standing. Her years of hard work began to take their toll, and after high blood pressure damaged her kidneys, Sarah weakened. The last words Madam Walker spoke were, *"I want to live to help my race."* It was reported by **The Chicago Defender**, that;

"... on Sunday morning, the day dawned bright and warm. Outside, where the trees and lawn were green and pretty, the flowers blooming and the birds merrily singing, all was gaiety and happiness. Inside, where several people gathered around a beautiful four-poster bed and watched a magnificent soul go into eternity, all was grief and sorrow."

On May 25, 1919, at the young age of 51, Sarah Breedlove Walker passed away. Thousands of mourners from all walks of life paid their respects as she was laid to rest at Woodlawn Cemetery with the reading of her favorite Bible passage, the 23rd Psalm.

In Indianapolis, we perhaps are more aware of Madam C.J. Walker and her contributions to all the world,

Original product box for one of Madam C.J. Walker's hair care items. Photos on both pages courtesy of A'Lelia Bundles..

"When indeed shall we learn that we are all related one to the other, that we are all members of one body? Until the spirit of love for our fellowmen, regardless of race, color or creed, shall fill the world, making real in our lives and our deeds the actuality of human brotherhood until great masses of the people shall be filled with the sense of responsibility for each other's welfare, social justice can never be attained."
Helen Keller

Sarah Breedlove "Madam C.J." Walker

Madam C.J. Walker driving her car down an Indianapolis street. Photo courtesy of A'Lelia Bundles.

came one of the most famous business-women of her time, leaving an estate valued at over a million dollars. She did not rest on her achievements; rather gave of herself and her money to improve others. She stated that,

"I was promoted from the cotton fields of the South, to the washtub, to the cook kitchen and then I promoted myself into the business of manufacturing. I have built my own factory on my own ground and I love to use a part of what I make in trying to help others."

therefore, I chose to design a quilt block in her honor and share her story with you. I find it encouraging that during the period Madam Walker lived, with the difficulties of a woman and even more so of an uneducated black woman, she was able to rise above all obstacles. Armed with an abundance of determination, she be-

Simple words from a simple woman speak volumes for what results can be achieved with hard work and determination. This woman of sparse beginnings possessed an uncommon amount of vision. Her rags to riches story should inspire women of all races that, if you Stand Up and Try, anything is possible.

Sarah's Song
By Kaye England
66" x 82"

"The true worth of a race must be measured by the character of its womanhood..."
Mary McLeod Bethune

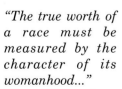

Sarah Breedlove "Madam C.J." Walker

Madame C.J. Walker
(12" Block)

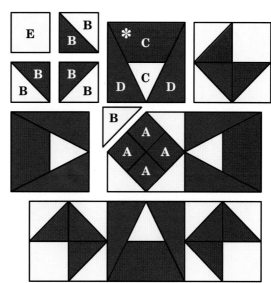

Piece	Fabric	Cut/Yield		Cutting Instructions
A	Medium	2		2" squares
A	Dark	2		2" squares
B	Light	8	16	2-7/8" sq. cut into half-square triangles
B	Dark	2	4	2-7/8" sq. cut into half-square triangles
B	Medium	4	8	2-7/8" sq. cut into half-square triangles
C*	Light	4		2-1/2 x 4-1/2" rectangles
C*	Medium	4		2-1/2 x 4-1/2" rectangles
D	Dark	8		4-1/2" square Connectors
E	Light	4		2-1/2" squares

Assemble block following piecing diagram above. See helpful piecing instructions in construction Tips & Advice. Quick piecing techniques can be used to simplify construction.

*Stitch Light C and Medium C, then add the Connectors.

Madame C.J. Walker
By Lydia Quigley of Ontario, Canada
46" x 46"

Madam C.J. Walker 32 cent stamp.

"I am a woman who came from the cotton fields of the South."
Madame C.J. Walker

Susan Brownell Anthony

**1820-1906
Social
Reformer**

Susan Brownell Anthony was born in Adams, Massachusetts February 15, 1820. Her father was a Quaker settling in Rochester, New York in 1846. From a father who opposed slavery, and from a Quaker meeting which taught equality before God, Susan Anthony gained a strong sense of independence and moral zeal that once drawn to the women's movement, devoted herself to it for over fifty years. Her education was in a private boarding school and her father encouraged her to get involved in reform movements to end or abolish slavery and to prohibit the sale and use of alcohol.

In 1846 Anthony became headmistress of the female department at Canajoharie Academy near Rochester, New York and was paid only a quarter as much as her male co-workers. The women teachers were not allowed to speak at teachers' meetings, even though they were behind the move-

"The day will come when men will recognize woman as his peer, not only at the fireside, but in the counsel of the nation."
Susan B. Anthony

ment to ban liquor. She taught for about ten years and then returned home to help with the family farm.

Anthony wasn't yet active in the movement but was angry that she or any woman could not speak in public. After hearing Lucy Stone speak in 1850 and being introduced to Elizabeth Cady Stanton by Amelia Bloomer, Susan B. Anthony dedicated her life to the women's movement. The life-long friendship of Stanton and Anthony kept them at the forefront of the women's movements for more than half a century.

Miss Anthony remained single although she did receive several proposals of marriage, believing that she would have the freedom to perform a roll impossible if married. Stanton was married and the mother of seven children. She spent hours writing powerful speeches and pamphlets that Anthony would take on the road. Although Anthony lacked the speaking ability of Stanton, she did most of the traveling encountering much abuse and violence on her trips.

Anthony was interested in the abolitionist movement, believing that until women's role was without limitations and they could vote, no results would be achieved. She and Stanton began a long campaign on behalf of women's suffrage and in 1860 New York passed a law that improved the rights of married women.

In 1869 they formed the National Woman Suffrage Association, the first national organization devoted primarily to women's suffrage. Their primary goal was to gain a Federal suffrage amendment. During the Civil War they obtained signatures supporting emancipation legislation but this brought them very little support for women's suffrage. After the Civil War with great hopes that both African

Susan Brownell Anthony

Americans and women would get the vote they were very disappointed with the results.

In 1872 Anthony was arrested for voting illegally in the presidential election and refused to pay the fine. Between 1870-1880 she lectured more than a hundred times a year from the north to the south. In 1871 alone she traveled over thirteen thousand miles and made over 170 speeches. In 1890 Stanton and Anthony formed the National American Woman Suffrage Association, dedicated to both a Federal amendment and State approval. During one meeting a minister told her; *"You are not married, You have no business to be discussing marriage."* *"Well,"* she replied, *"you are not a slave. Suppose you quit lecturing on slavery."*

By 1900 Anthony was recognized as a leader for her cause and at eighty she retired as president of the national association. At a convention in 1906 she rose and took her place at the podium to thank all of her colleagues for their loyal support. She had spent her life delivering long passionate talks but on this night she had a short message;

"There have been others also just as true and devoted to the cause - I wish I could name every one - but with such women consecrating their lives, failure is impossible!"

This would be Susan Anthony's final public work. She passed away shortly past midnight on March 13, 1906 with her sister Mary and friend Anna Howard Shaw by her side. It would be another fourteen years before women finally won the right to vote.

Throughout her life Anthony championed the causes of women's rights, temperance, abolition and labor, using every skill she had on hand to change the world.

Susan B. Anthony and Elizabeth Cady Stanton, 1898.

"Failure is impossible."
Susan B. Anthony

Susan Brownell Anthony

In accordance with the Quaker distaste for ceremonial mourning, sunlight streamed into the house and a wreath of violets decorated the front door. For two days friends and family came to call and the following day over ten thousand people faced a raging blizzard to say good-bye to this special person. A silk suffrage flag with four gold stars floated overhead representing the only states where women could vote and pinned on her breast was a jeweled flag pin with four diamond stars, a gift from the women of Wyoming, the first state to be enfranchised. Her friend Anna Howard Shaw delivered the final farewell at Anthony's bequest;

"There is no death for such as she. There are no last words of love. The ages to come will revere her name... Her words, her work and her character will go on to brighten the pathway and bless the lives of all peoples..."

A raging storm kept most people from the cemetery but beneath a simple white stone engraved with her name and date she was laid to rest in Mount Hope Cemetery in Rochester, New York. Susan B. Anthony had written her own epitaph during a family outing a few years earlier;

"When it is a funeral, remember that I want there should be no tears. Pass on, and go on with the work. "

Susan B. Anthony was an accomplished quilter and today a quilt she made in 1835 lives in the Susan B. Anthony house in Rochester. She delivered many of her messages at quilting bees because women were afraid to attend public meetings. Some women received their first information about their rights at these quilting bees. One of her interests was the Temperance Movement and she supported the Rochester women organizers of the WCTU, therefore I chose a variation of a curved two-patch similar to a Drunkard's Path block to honor Miss Anthony.

With the issue of a new dollar coin in 1979, she became the first real woman to be depicted on United States currency.

"Men their right and nothing more; women their right and nothing less."
Susan B. Anthony

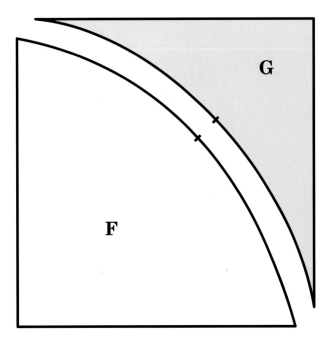

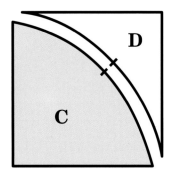

Add 1/4" seam allowance to each piece. Mark centers for easier piecing.

G

F

D

C

Susan Brownell Anthony

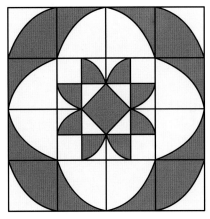

**Susan B. Anthony
(12" Block)**

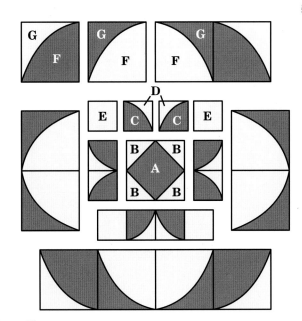

Piece	Fabric	Cut/Yield	Cutting Instructions
A	Dark	1	3-1/2" square
B	Light	4	2" square Connector Corners
C	Dark	8	Use Template C (on page 62)
D	Light	8	Use Template D (on page 62)
E	Light	4	2" squares
F	Light	8	Use Template F (on page 62)
F	Dark	4	Use Template F (on page 62)
G	Dark	8	Use Template G (on page 62)
G	Light	4	Use Template G (on page 62)

Assemble block following piecing diagram above. See helpful piecing instructions in Construction Tips & Advice.

Machine sew units with concave pieces (D and G) on bottom then ease (E and F) to fit their mates. Slow sewing allows the feed dogs to ease units together.

Freedom to Choose
*By Gachia Hoefer of Carmel, Indiana
52" x 62"*

"Give women the ballot, the political fulcrum, on which to plant her moral lever, and she will lift the world to a nobler and purer atmosphere."
Susan B. Anthony

Failure Is Impossible

Fabric Yardages

Main floral print	1 yard
Background	1 yard
Assorted Purples	1/4 yard
Assorted Greens	1/2 yard
Backing	2 yards
Binding	1/4 yard

Center Medallion

Make nine blocks following piecing diagram on page 63, see photo on this page for color placement.

Border One

Cut the following:

Background 12 3-1/2 x 6-1/2" rectangles
Background 4 3-1/2 x 3-1/2" squares
Background 24 Unit F
Greens 24 Unit G

Using templates F and G, make twelve curved two-patch units. Make strips as diagramed, connecting units with background strips. Attach shorter strips to sides and longer strips to top and bottom.

Border Two

Cut the following:
Asst. Purples 2 1-1/2" x 42-1/2" strips
Asst. Purples 2 1-1/2" x 44-1/2" strips
Attach strips to sides then to top and bottom. Make sure everything is square after every row.

Border Three

Cut the following:
Green fabric 2 2 x 44-1/2" strips
Green fabric 2 2 x 47-1/2" strips
Attach opposite sides, then top and bottom strips.

Border Four

Cut the following:
Asst. Purples 2 3-1/2 x 47-1/2" strips
Asst. Purples 2 3-1/2 x 53-1/2" strips
You know the routine, sides then top and bottom.

Finishing

Sandwich and quilt using your favorite technique.

Top and bottom strips

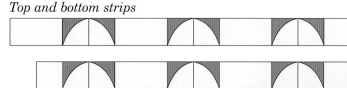

Sides strips

Failure is Impossible
By Candy Jewett of Belmont, Massachusetts Quilted by Loretta Pelletier 53" x 53"

The Alternate Blocks

*"In the older times it was seldom said to little girls,
as it always had been said to boys,
that they ought to have some definite plan,
while they were children,
what to be and do when they were grown up.*

*There was usually but one path open before them,
to become good wives and housekeepers.
And the ambition of most girls was to follow their
mother's footsteps in this direction;
a natural and laudable ambition.*

*But girls, as well as boys,
must often have been conscious of their own
peculiar capabilities-
must have desired to cultivate and make use of
their individual powers."*

Lucy Larcom

Aunt Dinah

Aunt Dinah
(12" Block)

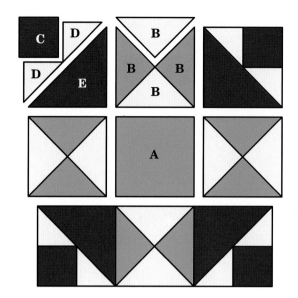

Piece Fabric Cut/Yield Cutting Instructions

Piece	Fabric	Cut	Yield	Cutting Instructions
A	Medium	1		4-1/2" square
B	Light	2	8	5-1/4" sq. cut into quarter-square triangles
B	Medium	2	8	5-1/4" sq. cut into quarter-square triangles
C	Dark	4		2-1/2" squares
D	Light	4	8	2-7/8" sq. cut into half-square triangles
E	Dark	2	4	4-7/8" sq. cut into half-square triangles

Assemble block following piecing diagram above. See helpful piecing instructions in Construction Tips & Advice. Quick pieced quarter-square triangles can be used to simplify construction of this block.

Aunt Dinah's Quilting Party

By Terri Gunn of
Indianapolis, Indiana
Quilted by Leona Berg
60" x 60"

In the sky the bright stars glittered
On the grass the moonlight shone;
From Aunt Dinah's quilting party
I was seeing Nellie home.

When the autumn tinged the greenwood,
Turning all its leaves to gold,
In the lawn by the elders shaded,
I my love to Nellie told.

As we stood together, gazing,
On the star-bespangled dome,
How I bless the August evening,
When I saw sweet Nellie home.
Stephen C. Foster

Eastern Star

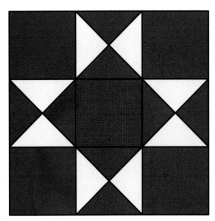

Eastern Star
(Ohio Star)
(7-1/2" Block)

Piece	Fabric	Cut/Yield		Cutting Instructions
A	Medium	1		3" square
A	Dark	4		3" squares
B	Light	2	8	3-3/4" sq. cut into quarter-square triangles
B	Dark	2	8	3-3/4" sq. cut into quarter-square triangles

Assemble block following piecing diagram above. See helpful piecing instructions in Construction Tips & Advice. Quick-pieced quarter-square triangles can be used to simplify construction of this block.

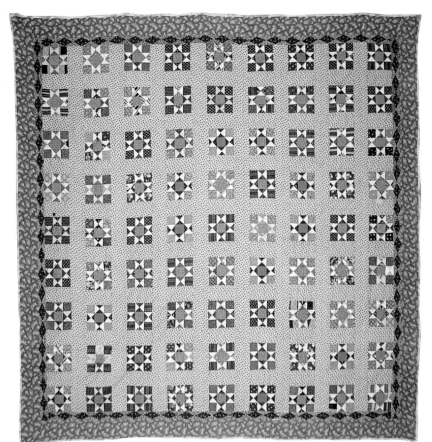

Easter Star
Antique quilt circa 1870
Collection of author
82" x 84"

"We never know how high we are till we are called to rise; and then, if we are true to plan our statures touch the sky."
Emily Dickinson

67

Baltimore Bell

Baltimore Bell
(Flying Geese)
(7-1/2" Block)

Piece	Fabric	Cut/Yield		Cutting Instructions
A	Dark	1		2-1/2" square
B	Dark	8		1-1/2 x 2-1/2" rectangles
C	Light	16		1-1/2" square Connector Corners
D	Dark	4		2" squares
E	Light	4	8	1-7/8" sq. cut into half-square triangles
F	Dark	1	4	5-3/4" sq. cut into quarter-square triangles

Assemble block following piecing diagram above. See helpful piecing instructions in Construction Tips & Advice. Quick cutting techniques are used on this block to simplify construction.

Baltimore Bell
Antique quilt circa 1875
Collection of author
65" x 78"

"Not knowing when the dawn will come I open every door."
Emily Dickinson

Baltimore Bell

Fabric Requirements

Asst'd Lights/Mediums	2 yards
Assorted Darks	3 yards
Setting Fabric	3 yards
Backing/Binding	4-3/4 yards

Blocks

Following piecing diagram on previous page, make thirty-six blocks of various colors as in photo.

Assembly

Cut the following:

Fabric	Cut/Yield		Cutting Instructions
Setting fabric	20	78	12" sq. cut into quarter-square setting triangles
Setting fabric	6	12	6-1/2" sq. cut into half-square corner triangles

Using the blocks and quarter-square setting triangles, make six rows of six blocks (see diagram to right). Use three setting triangles to square off one end, and use two half-square triangles to square off other end (see diagram).

You can trim down leaving 1/4" seam allowance or let the blocks "float" on the background fabric.

Alternate the strips top to bottom to offset blocks by a half-block.

Finishing

In reproducing this 1875 beauty I chose to finish the rows as the original maker had done. As the new maker, decide if you wish to add new borders or to do as this maker did, and only add borders at the top and bottom... the side border is only the binding. Perhaps this just fit her bed!

Half-square corner blocks   Quarter-square setting triangles

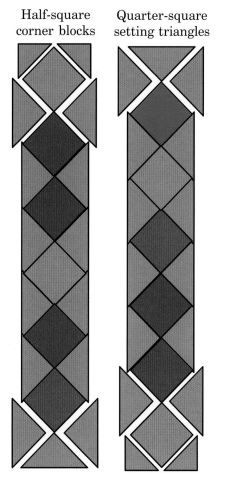

Strip of six blocks with setting triangles used to fill in sides of strip and one end. Half-square triangles are used to "square" off opposite end. Reverse for alternate rows.

"How pleasant it is, at the end of the day, no follies to have to repent; but reflect on the past, and be able to say, that my time has been properly spent."
Jane Taylor

Sister's Choice

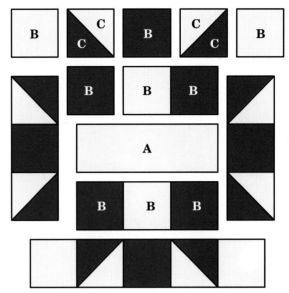

Sister's Choice
(10" Block)

Piece	Fabric	Cut/Yield		Cutting Instructions
A	Light	1		2-1/2 x 6-1/2" rectangle
B	Light	6		2-1/2" squares
B	Dark	8		2-1/2" squares
C	Light	4	8	2-7/8" sq. cut into half-square triangles
C	Dark	4	8	2-7/8" sq. cut into half-square triangles

Assemble block following piecing diagram above. See helpful piecing instructions in Construction Tips & Advice.

Sister's Choice
(Signature Quilt)
Antique quilt circa 1890
Collection of author
70" x 76"

Great-grandma made a "friendship quilt"
of scraps of calico,
Her neighbors gave small bits of cloth
from each new gown and sew
Great-grandma fashioned deftly
a quilt of cheerful hues,
And sewed with tiny stitches
the pink, and greys, and blues.
Elizabeth Yates

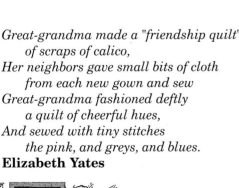

Sister's Choice

Fabric Requirements

Assorted Darks	2 yards
Assorted Backgrounds	3 yards
Background	3-1/2 yards

Blocks

Using assorted darks and backgrounds, make thirty-six blocks following piecing diagram on previous page.

Setting

Cut the following:

Fabric	Cut/Yield		Cutting Instructions
Background	25		10-1/2" squares
Background	5	20	10-1/2" sq. cut into quarter-square setting triangles
Background	2	4	10-1/2" sq. cut into half-square corner triangles

Follow diagram to right to make strips of blocks alternating with background squares.

Use setting triangles to fill out sides and corner triangles to square off top. Trim leaving 1/4" seam allowance all around.

Borders

Cut the following:

Fabric	Cut/Yield	Cutting Instructions
Dark fabric	2	2-1/2" x * strips
Background	2	2-1/2" x * strips

* length of finished quilt.

Attach dark strips to top an bottom of quilt top, then add background strips to top and bottom.

Finish

Sandwich, quilt and bind using a dark fabric.

A Tip from Kaye

A great quilt for a special gift for a family member or friend or group activities at school, church or other civic groups. I encourage you to gather signatures on the center strips before you begin. That way you'll know how many you have to make and, heaven forbid, someone makes a mistake... on your finished quilt!

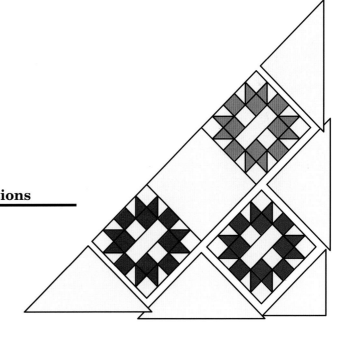

"Talk happiness, the world is sad enough without your woe, no past is wholly rough."
Ella Wheeler Wilcox

Chelsea's Basket

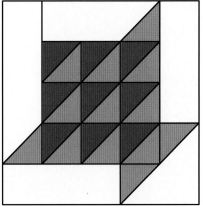

**Chelsea's Basket
(10" Block)**

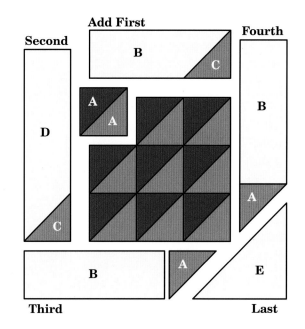

Piece Fabric Cut/Yield Cutting Instructions

Piece	Fabric	Cut	Yield	Cutting Instructions
A	Medium	5	9	2-7/8" sq. cut into half-square triangles
A	Dark	6	11	2-7/8" sq. cut into half-square triangles
B	Light	3		2-1/2 x 6-1/2" rectangles
C	Medium	2		2-1/2" sq. Connector Corners
D	Light	1		2-1/2 x 8-1/2" rectangle
E	Light	1	1	4-7/8" sq. cut into half-square triangles

Assemble block following piecing diagram above. See helpful piecing instruction in Construction Tips & Advice. Quick piecing techniques are used to simplify construction.

Chelsea's Basket

*Antique quilt circa 1880
Collection of the author
68" x 78"*

Unable to find a name for this block. I named it for my first grand-daughter, Chelsea Kaye Richards.

"The future belongs to those who believe in the beauty of their dreams."
Eleanor Roosevelt

Chelsea's Basket

Fabric Requirements

Background	1 yard
Medium fabric	3/4 yard
Dark fabric (+binding)	1 yard
Backing	1-1/4 yard

Blocks

Following piecing diagram on opposite page, make five blocks. See photo at right for color placement.

On-Point Setting

Fabric	Cut/Yield		Cutting Instructions
Background	1	4	16" sq. cut into quarter-square setting triangles (sides)

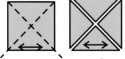

Background	2	4	9" sq. cut into half-square corner triangles

Following diagram at right, layout blocks in an "on-point" setting, using setting triangles at sides, top and bottom to even out the edges. Use the corner triangles to "square" up the quilt top. Trim to 28-1/2" square.

Border One

Fabric	Cut/Yld		Cutting Instructions
Medium	30	60	2-7/8" sq. cut into half-sq. triangles
Dark	30	60	2-7/8" sq. cut into half-sq. triangles

Join into strips following diagram at right.

Border Two

Fabric	Cut/Yld		Cutting Instructions
Medium	18	36	4-7/8" sq. cut into half-sq. triangles
Dark	18	36	4-7/8" sq. cut into half-sq. triangles

Join into strips following diagram at right.

Border Three

Fabric	Cut/Yld	Cutting Instructions
Floral	2	2-1/2 x 40-1/2" strips
Floral	2	2-1/2 x 44-1/2" strips

Attach short strips to top and bottom, longer strips to sides.

Finishing

Quilt and enjoy!

Chelsea's Basket
By Kaye England
44" x 44"

Old Maid's Ramble

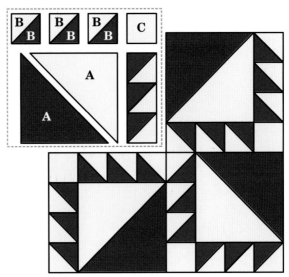

Old Maid's Ramble
(12" Block)

Piece	Fabric	Cut	Yield	Cutting Instructions	
A	Light	2	4	5-3/8" sq. cut into half-square triangles	Assemble block following piecing diagram above. See helpful piecing instructions in Construction Tips & Advice.
A	Dark	2	4	5-3/8" sq. cut into half-square triangles	
B	Light	12	24	2-3/8" sq. cut into half-square triangles	
B	Dark	12	24	2-3/8" sq. cut into half-square triangles	
C	Light	4		2" squares	

Old Maid's Ramble

By Terri Gunn of Indianapolis, Indiana 36" x 36"

"I do not ask for any crown but that which all may win; never to try to conquer any world except the one within. Be thou my guide until I find led by a tender hand, the happy kingdom in myself and dare to take command."
Louisa May Alcott

Old Maid's Ramble

Fabric Requirements

Plaid fabric (borders)	3/4 yard
Assorted Backgrounds	3/4 yard
Red fabric	1/3 yard
Assorted plaids	3/4 yard
Backing	1 yard

Center

Following piecing diagram on page 74, make four Old Maid's Ramble blocks. Join into a square as in photo.

Border One

Fabric	Cut/Yld	Cutting
Red fabric	2	1-1/4 x 24-1/2" strips
Red fabric	2	1-1/4 x 26" strips

Attach shorter strips to sides and longer strips to top and bottom.

Border Two

Fabric	Cut/Yld	Cutting
Plaids	36 72	2-3/8" sq. cut into half-sq. triangles
Backgrounds	36 72	2-3/8" sq. cut into half-sq. triangles

Join plaids and backgrounds to form half-square units, make into strips and attach.

Border Three

Fabric	Cut/Yld	Cutting
Red fabric	2	1-1/4 x 29" strips
Red fabric	2	1-1/4 x 30-1/2" strips

Attach shorter strips to opposite sides and longer strips to top and bottom.

Border Four

Fabric	Cut/Yld	Cutting
Plaid border	2	3-1/2 x 30-1/2" strips
Plaid border	2	3-1/2 x 36-1/2" strips

Attach shorter strips to opposite sides and longer strips to top and bottom.

Finishing

Quilt and bind using your favorite techniques.

"You may search my time-worn face,
You will find a merry eye that twinkles,
I am Not an old lady
Just a little girl with wrinkles."
Edythe E. Bregnard

School Girl's Puzzle

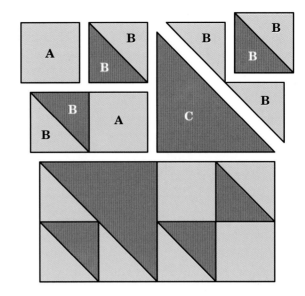

School Girl's Puzzle
(8" Block)

Piece	Fabric	Cut	Yield	Cutting Instructions
A	Light	4		2-1/2" squares
B	Light	5	10	2-7/8" sq. cut into half-square triangles
B	Dark	3	6	2-7/8" sq. cut into half-square triangles
C	Dark	1	2	4-7/8" sq. cut into half-square triangles

Assemble following the piecing diagram above. See helpful piecing instructions in Constucion Tips & Advice.

School Girl's Puzzle
Antique quilt circa 1880
Collection of author
82" x 87"

"Once the children were in the house, the air became more vivid and more heated; every object in the house grew more alive."
Mary Jordan

School Girl's Puzzle

Fabric Requirements

Assorted Darks	1-3/4 yards
Assorted Medium/Lights	1-3/4 yard
Sashing/Borders/Binding	4-1/2 yard

Applique Fabrics

Dark fabric	1/8 yard
Print fabric	1/4 yard
Medium fabric	1/2 yard
Backing	6 yards

Center Blocks

Following piecing diagram on opposite page, create thirty blocks. See photo for color suggestions and placement.

Sashing

Fabric	Cut	Cutting
Sashing	24	4 x 8-1/2" strips
Sashing	5	4 x 54-1/2" strips

Join blocks into columns using sashing strips between blocks. Join these columns with long sashing strips to create center of quilt.

Outer Border

Fabric	Cut	Cutting
Border	2	14-1/2 x 54-1/2" sides
Border	1	14-1/2 x 82-1/2" bottom
Border	1	8 x 82-1/2" top strip

Attach 54-1/2" long strips to opposite sides, then the narrow border to top and wider border to bottom.

Applique

Fabric	Cut	Cutting
Dark print	36	(Berries)
Print fabric	36	(Leaves)
Medium fabric	17	(Vines)
Medium fabric	2	(Corner Vines)

See templates on following pages. Using your favorite applique technique sew the above pieces to wide borders of quilt top. Baste pieces to background fabric to secure them in place while appliqueing.

Finishing

Quilt and bind your new quilt top. Enjoy!

School Girl's Puzzle
By Charity Millard Brown
Antique quilt circa 1860
Collection of author
82" x 87"

"Young people do not know enough to be prudent and therefore they attempt the impossible and achieve it, generation after generation."
Pearl S. Buck

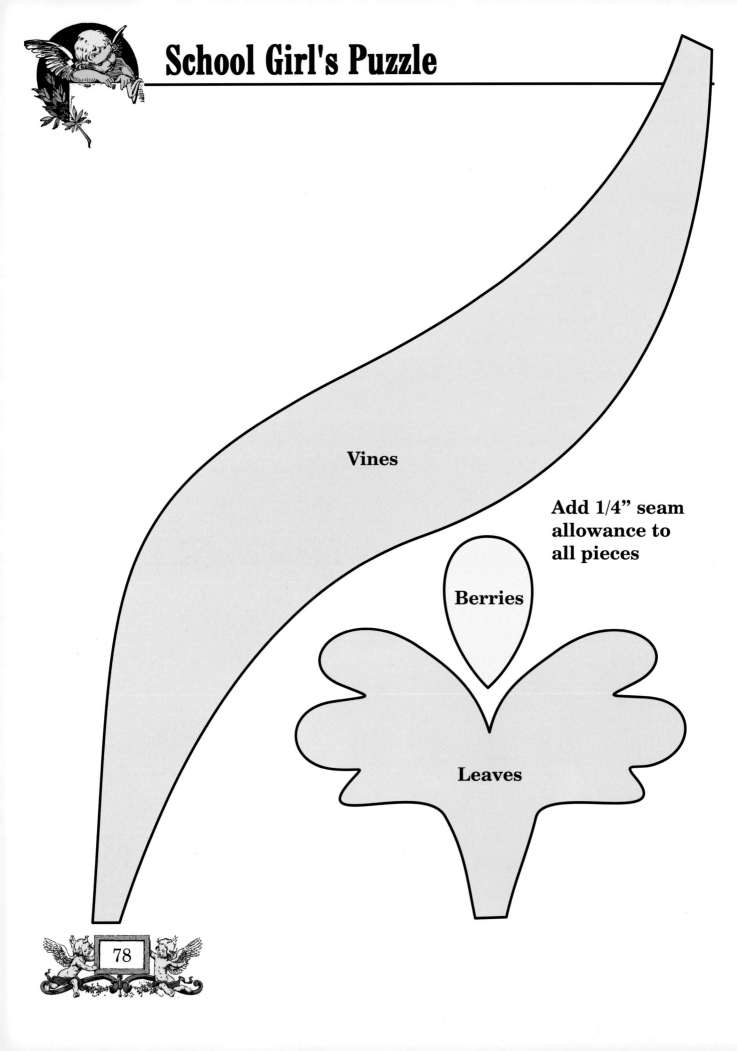

School Girl's Puzzle

Vines

Add 1/4" seam
allowance to
all pieces

Berries

Leaves

School Girl's Puzzle

**Corner
Vines**

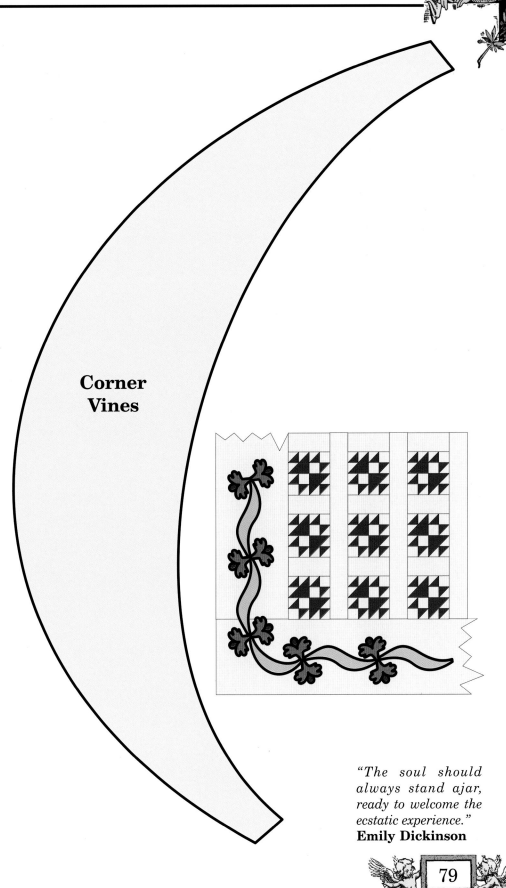

*"The soul should
always stand ajar,
ready to welcome the
ecstatic experience."*
Emily Dickinson

Mother's Crown

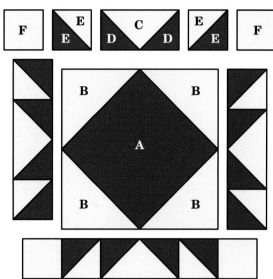

Mother's Crown
(9" Block)

Piece	Fabric	Cut/Yield		Cutting Instructions
A	Dark	1		6-1/2" square
B	Light	4		3-1/2" square Connector Corners
C	Light	4		2 x 3-1/2" rectangles
D	Dark	8		2" square Connector Corners
E	Light	4	8	2-3/8" sq. cut into half-square triangles
E	Dark	4	8	2-3/8" sq. cut into half-square triangles
F	Light	4		2" squares

Assemble block following piecing diagram above. Notice the difference, the blocks are set "on-point" below and straight set on the opposite page.

Mother's Crown
Antique quilt circa 1880
Collection of the author
82" x 86"

"No woman has a right to put a stitch of ornament on any article of dress or furniture... until she is sure she can secure time for all her social, intellectual benevolent and religious duties."
Catherine E. Beecher and Harriet Beecher Stowe
The American Woman's Home, 1869

Construction Tips & Advice

Mother's Crown
By Kaye England
40" x 60"

Mother's Day Proclamation

Arise, then, women of this day! Arise all women who have hearts, whether your baptism be that of water or of fears!
Say firmly: We will not have great questions decided by irrelevant agencies,
Our husbands shall not come to us reeking with carnage, for caresses and applause.
Our sons shall not be taken from us to unlearn all that we have been able to teach them of charity, mercy. and patience
We women of one country will be too tender of those of another country to allow our sons to be trained to injure theirs.
From the bosom of the devastated earth a voice goes up with our own.
It says, "Disarm, Disarm!"
The sword of murder is not the balance of justice!
Blood does not wipe our dishonor nor violence indicate possession.
As men have often forsaken the plow and the anvil at the summons of war.
Let women now save all that may be left of home for a great and earnest day of counsel.
Let them meet first, as women, to bewail and commemorate the dead.
Let them then solemnly take counsel with each other as the means whereby the great human family can live in peace,
And each bearing after her own time the sacred impress, not of Caesar, but of God."
Julia Ward Howe

Julia Ward Howe first suggested a Mother's Day in the United States in 1872. In 1907 Anna Jarvis began a campaign for a nationwide observance of Mother's Day. The second Sunday in May was chosen and a custom of wearing a carnation on that day began. A colored carnation means that a person's mother is living and a white carnation means that a person's mother is deceased.

Thoughts

As you study the twenty blocks furnished in this book, spend some time looking at each of the quilts. You will quickly see that a variety of outcomes were achieved by the makers color and value choices. At this time I also like to consider setting options such as will it be a straight set, diagonal, strippie, medallion or whatever you decide. This decision helps me in determining fabrics because if I decided to do twelve blocks set without sashings, I might give some thought to changing fabrics in corners to create a secondary design. For instance, a block with four corner squares might have two corners blue and the other two pink, then when the block was set with it's neighbor you would have a *free* four patch as shown. Looking for secondary designs makes this piecing process a real challenge. Mary

Secondary Designs

Ellen Hopkins has long been a staunch supporter of the lowly simple blocks because the secondary designs are so wonderful. Give it a Try.

I truly believe you can make an incredible nine-patch with the right fabrics and if you would agree then certainly fabric choices will be your first decision. After viewing all of the quilts make your decision and get busy. As you will see from most of my quilts, I prefer working with a variety of fabrics. It's a great chance to work with your stash and I think the resulting quilts are really interesting. I tend to have the strongest reactions to quilts that require some time to take it all in. This is made possible with the variety of fabric, because regardless of the complexity of a design, it seems to be the fabric that gets the strongest reaction.

To Wash or Not to Wash:

I should know better than to touch this subject but I'm going to give you my opinion and then you will have to decide for yourself. If you read all the material published on this subject my guess is you will still be confused because there are such conflicting reports, therefore I have arrived at what works for me. I never pre-wash my fabric before piecing. Now, after you are revived, read on. I can make this statement because I'm very aware of the fabric I'm working with and if I am ever in doubt, I will do a test to see if there is any bleeding. I prefer to do all my testing in cold water because that's all I'm ever going to use on my quilts. I see no sense in testing in hot water when I would never wash my quilt in hot water. I have made quite a few quilts and just simply have not had

a problem with this. Now if you are a bargain hunter in your fabric search you had better be more aware because in most cases, if it's cheap there's a reason. I like a good buy like everyone else, I simply encourage you to be an informed buyer and you will avoid most of these pitfalls. If for some reason you just have to wash your fabrics, then use Orvus™ soap and cool or cold water.

Other than the time it takes to wash fabrics, my other reason is I simply prefer to work with fabric that still has the sizing intact. I think it's much easier to handle than softer pre-washed fabrics. Like all things, you must decide for yourself, however if you add up all that time it takes to wash, dry, iron, fold, etc., you could have made a few blocks.

Construction Tips & Advice

Sewing Machine

All of the blocks included in this project piece very easily on the machine. You could certainly hand piece them if you choose. If you are machine piecing, it is essential that you have a machine that is in good working condition. You really don't need lots of fancy stuff (although it's great fun), just basic straight stitch will do a super job of piecing all of these blocks. I am fanatical about changing needles and keeping the machine clean and oiled. I also highly recommend that you have your machine professionally clean on an annual basis. Once your machine is healthy, I also highly recommend that you piece with cotton thread. Think about it, you're using 100% cotton fabric, why not 100% cotton thread. Now so far I have my fabric, a clean happy machine and my cotton thread. What next; Oh yes, if at all possible look for a single needle throat plate for your machine. You'll spend lots less time fishing your small triangles out of that hole in the zigzag plate. I couldn't believe the difference this made in my work. I also prefer to use fabric tails to start and stop my sewing. In other words I never have dangling threads because I just use scraps to feed at the end then reach to the back and cut away my work always leaving a scrap under the needle. This does take some getting use to but you will be shocked at the time you save from clipping threads and re-threading. Now we're ready to get to the real test.

Rotary Cutting Tips

Once I used this tool, I was forever hooked on this method of cutting my pieces. The speed and accuracy afforded by these tools has revolutionized quiltmaking. Take great care in handling these cutters as they can be very dangerous. I really encourage everyone to make it a habit to close the cutter after each cut to avoid injury. Like all things, there are many opinions of what's correct. My main goal is to have accurate strips (without those nasty humps in the middle) because if you go awry here, all remaining tasks just get tougher.

I prefer to make my first cut with the fold facing toward my body and if you are right handed, the excess fabric should always be to your right for this first cut. I've seen some pretty interesting contorted movements to get that first cut completed. I pretty much use the fold as it comes off the bolt, disregarding grain for the most part. If I am planning a 3" cut, I would make the first cut over 3", then simply turn that one piece over and re-cut to size. This keeps you from flipping all that yardage or running around the table or having your friend on the other side of the table cut for you. Thank you for admitting that you do some of these things. After I make the first cut, I have no problem folding up again and cutting through four layers. Be sure you have a good sharp blade and this is a piece of cake. I've become really fond of the jumbo cutter as it requires a shorter stroke.

Construction Tips & Advice

Rulers

This could be an entire book, but again my opinion...

I have a couple of favorite rulers, but regardless of the brand you choose, I recommend you stay within that brand for the most part. If I use brand *X* for my 6 x 24", then I would stay with that brand for my 6" squares, etc. I think it makes your work more accurate to do so. I do have my favorite speciality rulers as I'm sure you do and regardless of the brand you have chosen, it's success for you that counts. If you are not having good results, visit your local quilt shop for a demo on the wide variety available. I really like the 12 or 15 inch square rulers for cleaning up my corners and cutting larger blocks.

Even though we have this huge variety of speciality rulers, I think you need to know the good old traditional methods for calculating various units. If you were to lose all of your special rulers you could still make any of these projects if you are armed with the following information.

Squares and Rectangles

I prefer to cut a strip of either the width or length of my unit, then cut this strip into the desired units. Need a 2-1/2" square (finished)? Cut a strip 3" x the length of the fabric. Now you just cut this strip down into as many 3" lengths as you can.

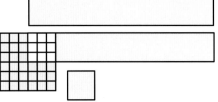
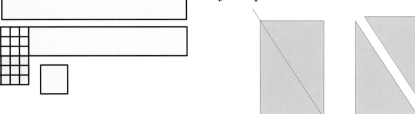

Half Square Triangles

The traditional method for calculating this unit is to know the finished size of the shortest leg (finished size), and add 7/8" to this measurement, cut a square, then crosscut on the diagonal to yield two triangles. This is the same method used to cut corner triangles for use in diagonal sets.

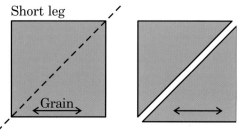

Quarter Square Triangles

This triangle is calculated using the finished measurement of the long leg (which would provide straight of grain on the outside edge), adding 1-1/4", cutting a square, then cutting diagonally twice.

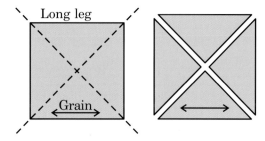

Bias Rectangles

I prefer to piece this unit as a connector but to cut traditionally you would need to know the finished size of the unit and then add 5/8" to the width and 1 1/4" to the length. Cutting from corner to corner on the diagonal would yield perfect units.

Construction Tips & Advice

Gridding Triangles

This is a real timesaver! Determine the finished size of your triangles and add 7/8". This will set the size of your drawn squares. Mark grids on the back of the lightest fabric (A & B). Beginning at the upper left square, mark a line from upper right to lower left (C), skip a square then mark another line from point 3 to point 4 and from point 5 to point 6.

Repeat this process starting at upper righthand square (D). Lay marked fabric onto second fabric, right-sides together and pin as marked (E).

Start at lower left, sew 1/4" from marked line all the way around the grid (F), repeat on other side of line (G). Cut triangles on all marked lines horizontal, vertical and diagonal (H). In this example you'll get 24 finished half-square triangle units (I)!

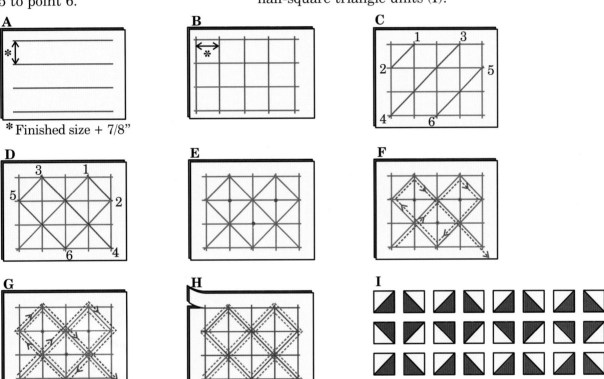

* Finished size + 7/8"

Connector Corners

There are many other sizes that can successfully be cut with your basic rulers but I think these are the units you would need to piece the blocks in this book. Having addressed the traditional methods, I would introduce you to my most favorite way to piece when at all possible and that is the Connector Method developed by Mary Ellen Hopkins almost twenty years ago. Many successful teachers are using Mary Ellen's methods and I highly recommend you give these a try. Most of the directions in this book are writ-

ten using this technique when possible. You simply lay a Connector square on a base square (or strip) right sides together and stitch diagonally from corner to corner, fold back, press and trim out the middle layer only. This yields a perfect triangle and if you leave the base fabric intact you are less likely to get out of square.

For more information on this, refer to Mary Ellen Hopkins' ***Connecting Up*** book or my ***Winter Wonderland*** book.

Bias Rectangle Connectors

Jackie Kennedy, Sojourner Truth and Madam C.J. Walker blocks all use this technique and it makes quick work of this pesky unit.

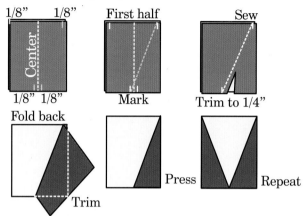

Bias Rectangles are sewn as illustrated

Cut the base fabric the finished size of your unit plus seam allowance. On back side of fabric mark center of bottom edge. Make a mark 1/8" to each side of this mark. Now make a mark 1/8" from left and right edges on top edge. Draw a line from the top-edge mark on the left to the bottom edge mark that is 1/8" to the right of center (see drawing). Repeat for mark on the right edge. Lay this marked unit on the bias connector fabric piece (right-sides together), sew on one line, then press back and trim inside layer only. When finished sewing, trim to excess fabric to edges of base square. Repeat for other side. This method of piecing bias rectangles is time saving and really creates great results.

I have included a separate drawing on the Jackie Kennedy block to simplify one of the units. This method really doesn't add a measurable amount of bulk and assures you perfect points.

Templates

I have included templates for Susan B. Anthony block and applique patterns for Schoolgirl's Puzzle. I prefer to make templates as follows:

Trace the pattern onto a piece of template material (translucent plastic) using a fine line pen or pencil. Add a quarter-inch seam allowance around the template.

Punch a hole in the template (with 1/8" hole puncher, available at most office supply stores) at seam intersections. Place the template on the wrong side of the fabric, being aware of grain-line and trace around the template. Mark seam intersections through holes in template and connect the marks (seam lines).

Align seam intersection using the marks and sew on lines between marks. Be sure to use good scissors (or rotary cutter if you wish) to cut your fabric.

I also have great success using freezer-paper if I only need to use it a few times. When you are piecing the Anthony block I recommend you piece with the concave piece on the bottom. You can ease the convex piece easier much like easing a sleeve into a casing. I generally do not need to clip on these pieces.

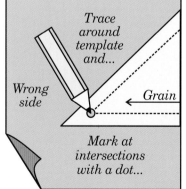

Punch 1/8" hole in template at intersections

Grain

Trace around template and...

Wrong side

Grain

Mark at intersections with a dot...

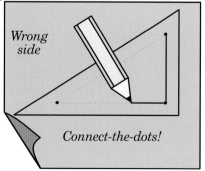

Wrong side

Connect-the-dots!

Construction Tips & Advice

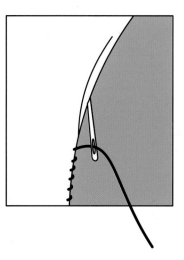

Needle-Turn Applique

Even though we have only included a few applique patterns I think it's always good to have another look at this technique.

There are so many great applique books on the market that I hope you find time to study them. I find this is a tough topic to cover in just a few paragraphs. There are so many ways to applique, but for this project I will discuss needle-turn only.

Unlike piecing, your applique shape is marked on the right side of the fabric with the sewing line visible, forcing you to turn under the seam allowances as you go. I prefer to use a #11 sharp needle for applique and thread to match the piece. Bring the needle up and through the back of the fabric and through the fold of the top fabric, passing back down slightly ahead of the previous stitch. Small stitches no more than 1/8" are desirable. With the tip of the needle, turn under as you move around the pattern piece.

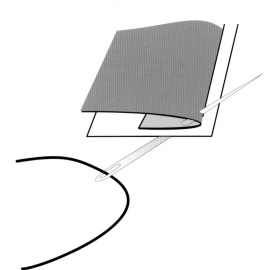

Pressing

To steam or not to steam, that is the question. I say steam if you want weird shaped pieces, otherwise don't steam. Steam is like a vice we have... used in moderation it's okay, but overused it is deadly. Most people iron as if they were really mad at the fabric and therefore can completely change the shape without realizing it. A dry iron has less chance to distort your piecing, especially if working with bias edges. Remember to let the iron glide by itself and not to ride on it. In our classes, we teach how to make rainbows out of triangles. It's real easy with steam. If you prefer working with steam, by all means do so, just be careful and be aware of the dangers. When pressing applique, I prefer to press face down in a towel and then I use steam, but not to excess.

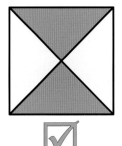 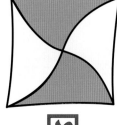

Outside and Corner Triangles

For the outside triangles, cut squares with sides equal to the main block diagonal measurement plus 3". Cut these into quarters.

For the corner triangles, cut squares equal to the blocks diagonal plus 1/2". Cut these on the diagonal. Attach these as appropriate to the ends of the di-agonal rows of main blocks and alternate blocks., For further information refer to Mary Ellen Hopkins' ***It's Okay If You Sit On My Quilt***.

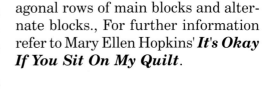

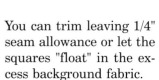

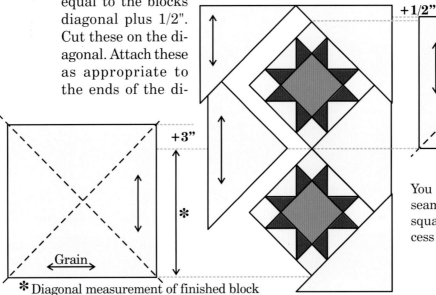

You can trim leaving 1/4" seam allowance or let the squares "float" in the excess background fabric.

* Diagonal measurement of finished block

Making the Sandwich

To sandwich your quilt lay prepared back face down on a flat surface. (For my back, I choose to sew strips on each side of the larger piece, this way I have two seams down the back, rather than one down the center.)

Have a friend help you smooth the back and then masking tape it down. Place batt on back and then add the quilt top face up. Make sure your back and batt are larger than the top.

Baste from the center to the opposite sides, then from center to top and bottom, continue from center to corners.

You may use large running stitches for this. (Tip: start at center with a long thread, baste to one side, leaving enough thread at the center to re-thread needle and baste to the opposite side.) If necessary, put basting stitches be-tween these lines, always radiating out in the one direction, then the opposite. An alternate approach is to always start at the center with a backstitch baste outward.

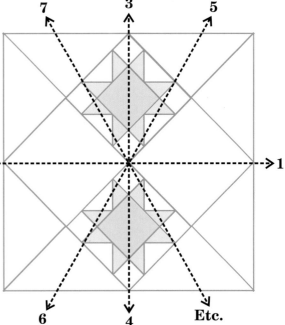

Construction Tips & Advice

Applying Borders

There are two types of borders. Square borders can be applied by attaching pieces to two opposite sides, of the quilt. To determine the length of these pieces, measure across the quilt at its center. Next, measure across the other dimension of the quilt including the previously attached borders, again at the center of the quilt. Cut border pieces of this length and attach them to the remaining two sides of the quilt.

Mitered borders are more appropriate if you will be appliqueing in the border or using a stripe. Attach border strips to all sides, using a length equal to the quilt dimension plus two border widths plus seam allowances, don't sew borders to each other yet. Fold the quilt top right-sides together over a 45 degree angle, mark at the corner to be mitered. Sew borders at the the 45 degree angle and trim.

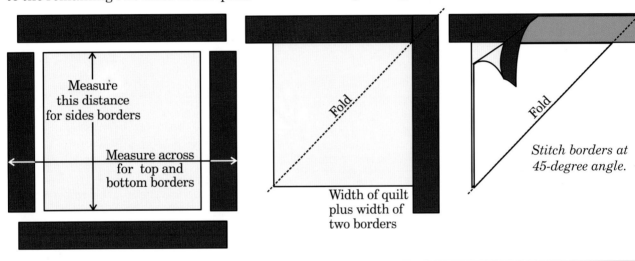

Measure this distance for sides borders

Measure across for top and bottom borders

Fold

Width of quilt plus width of two borders

Fold

Stitch borders at 45-degree angle.

Applying the Binding

Cut the strips of bias fabric 2-1/2". Fold in half (don't press), and sew to the front edge of the sandwiched quilt, aligning raw edges to the outside (1/4" seam). Fold the binding over the seam to the back of the quilt and whip stitch into place. Cut bindings on the bias if it is necessary to do so (for example, to make a stripe go a certain way), otherwise I usually don't cut on the bias.

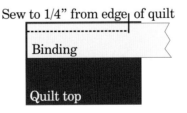

To attach the binding at the corners, sew the binding on as indicated above sewing to within 1/4" of the corner. Turn the binding up, folding at a

45 degree angle. Then fold the binding down over the top of this fold to the edge of the binding is even with the top of the quilt and the side. Continue sewing from the corner.

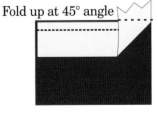

Sew to 1/4" from edge of quilt

Binding

Quilt top

Fold up at 45° angle

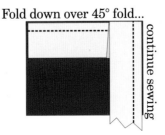

Fold down over 45° fold...

continue sewing

Quilting

Quilting will finish your quilt by adding depth and dimensions to the designs or creating designs complementing your piecing. Quilting is simply the same running stitch except through three layers instead of one. I really feel you should try to quilt with nothing smaller than a #10 Between needle. If you use a larger needle it becomes more difficult to achieve tiny even stitches. You should practice keeping your stitches even, top and bottom – I prefer larger, even stitches to small, uneven ones. As in most things, if you have a plan that works for you, then stay with it.

Use a small length of thread to quilt, no longer than 18". When hand quilting I choose to avoid knotting the thread. I feel if you can pop the knot through to start, sometime during the quilt's life it will pop back out. Instead I float the needle and backstitch before quilting then backstitch and float when I end a thread.

To float the needle, start by inserting the length of needle through the top into the batt (not through the back!). Bring the needle out until only the eye is still inside the quilt. Turn the needle point back away from the direction of quilting, and , with your thimble, push the eye end of the needle forward in the batt another length of the needle. Bring the needle back out, eye first, but not all the way. You will have floated the needle two needle lengths and may continue in this way, or if starting a thread, you may backstitch and begin. If prefer to have approximately 3" of thread floating at the start and end of a quilting thread. This will leave the tail in between layers and you can hardly pull this out. Before I backstitch at the beginning of a thread, I pull the loose end into the quilt. After backstitching and floating the needle at the end of the thread, I pull it taut and cut it, forcing the thread to pull back into the quilt.

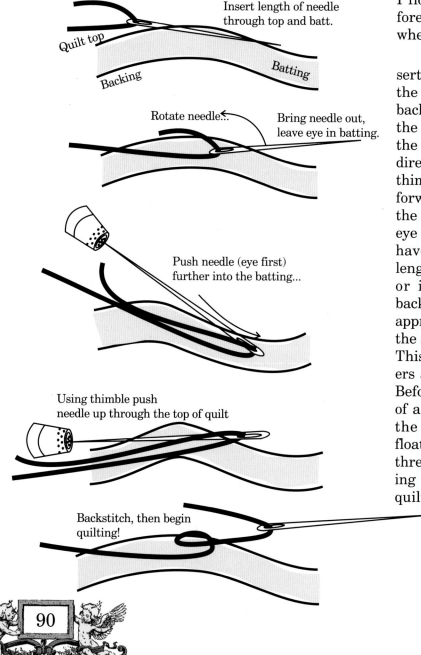

Insert length of needle through top and batt.

Quilt top

Backing

Batting

Rotate needle...

Bring needle out, leave eye in batting.

Push needle (eye first) further into the batting...

Using thimble push needle up through the top of quilt

Backstitch, then begin quilting!

Construction Tips & Advice

Machine Quilting

While I recognize many quilters still believe that the only quilting acceptable is hand quilting, I encourage you to try machine quilting. It offers a greater opportunity to give your loved ones quilts in your lifetime and I believe it requires as much talent to be a great machine quilter as a great hand quilter. I will not debate which method has the greatest value as I believe it is in the eyes of the beholder. I like both methods, believe both methods have their place and am happily using both methods. My favorite analogy on this is, few of you are still pounding the clothes on rocks in a stream, so relax and give it a try. I highly recommend Harriet Hargrave's ***Heirloom Machine Quilting*** book on this subject.

Quilt Care and Fabric Care

We could discuss this subject for months and months and still not agree on the final results. I do not wash my fabric before use, but I do test for colorfastness. This is such an important topic, I prefer to tell you what I do and then have you make your own choices. I again highly recommend, ***Heirloom Machine Quilting*** by Harriet Hargrave. She has a textile background and thoroughly discusses this topic in her book. I think a lot of questions have gone unanswered until now on the care of textiles. As in all things, you must do what works for you, but I just can't make myself wash fabric that isn't dirty!

Backing

I really think backs are fast becoming another quilt as many quilters put considerable time in the backside of their creation. I rarely take the time to be really creative, but do love seeing other peoples' results.

If I have a piece that is just a tad wider than one width of fabric, I like to just add a strip of another fabric instead of piecing with the same fabric. What is it with us, we have zillions of yards but just can't seem to waste it. Keep in mind that with all the work you have in the front side some time should be spent on this large consideration for your quilt.

Documenting Your Work

Above all, when you have finished your project, be sure and sign it. Document it with a label containing all information. As an avid collector of antique quilts, I always yearn to have more information than was provided, but it's lost forever, because the maker did not sign the work. I know that if you don't do this when you put that last stitch in the binding, you'll be like me and they mount up and you never get it done. Try making the labels fun and part of the project. Truly, the label can be an additional art form if you choose. I try to include as much information

In Honor of My First Grandchild!
Shaniqua
Born August 27, 1998
To My Daughter,
Mimi
Love, Mom
(Tipper du Frie, 1998)

on the label, such as name, location, the name of the recipient if known, and if it was for a special reason. The person who has this project in 2099 is the one that will really appreciate this documentation. Look for cutouts you can fuse to a label to specialize your work even more. You'll love the finished results.

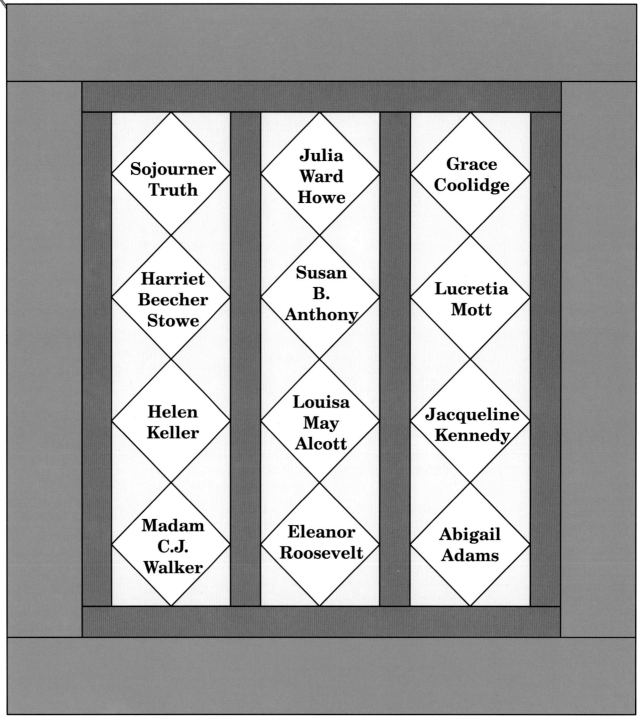

Living the Legacy

Each block has a finished size of 12". Make strips of four blocks set on-point using setting triangles and corners to square off rows. The rows are then set together with sashing strips and finished with a wide border. See color photo on page 4.

Construction Tips & Advice

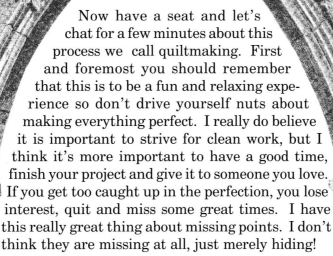

Now have a seat and let's chat for a few minutes about this process we call quiltmaking. First and foremost you should remember that this is to be a fun and relaxing experience so don't drive yourself nuts about making everything perfect. I really do believe it is important to strive for clean work, but I think it's more important to have a good time, finish your project and give it to someone you love. If you get too caught up in the perfection, you lose interest, quit and miss some great times. I have this really great thing about missing points. I don't think they are missing at all, just merely hiding!

I get great pleasure out of my piecing and really strive to do good work but sometimes it just doesn't work that way and I just move on and learn from the experience. Most of my treasured antique quilts are not perfect pieced projects but they are still highly prized. If you are planning to exhibit your work, then certainly clean work is necessary. Please don't think I am encouraging sloppy piecing, I just think life is too short to spend it moaning over a few lost points. Regardless of your approach, my wish is that you would have countless hours of fun piecing and wonderful reading in this project.

Kaye's Sermon

Bibliography

Anthony, Carl Sferrazza; *First Ladies*; Morrow and Company, New York, 1990

Bacon, Margaret Hope; *Valiant Friend*; Walker & Company, New York, 1980

Bank, Mirra; *Anonymous Was a Woman*; St. Martens Press, New York, 1979

Barry, Kathleen; *Susan B. Anthony, A Biography*; New York University Press, New York, 1988

Bobbe, Dorothie; *Abigail Adams, The Second First Lady;* Minton, Balch & Co., New York, 1929

Brooks, Gertrude Zeth; *First Ladies of the White House;* Hallberg & Co, Chicago, 1969

Brooks, Van Wyck; *Helen Keller*; Dutton & Co., New York, 1956

Bryant, Jennifer Fisher; *Lucretia Mott, A Guiding Light*; Eedmans Publishing Company,Michigan 1996

Bundles, A 'Lelia Perry; *Madam C. J. Walker Entrepreneur*, Chelsea House, New York, 1991

Cook, Blanche Wiesen; *Eleanor Roosevelt;* Viking Press, New York, 1992

Finley, Ruth E.; *Old Patchwork Quilts*; Branford Company, Massachusetts, 1929

Garko, Miriam; *The Ladies of Seneca Falls*, Schocke Books, New York, 1974

Hall, Carrie & Kretsinger, Rose; *The Romance of the Patchwork Quilting in America*; Bonanza Books, New York, 1933

Hargrave, Harriet; *Heirloom Machine Quilting*; C & T Publishing, Lafayette, California, 1990

Harper & Brothers Publishers; *Collected Lyrics of Edna St. Vincent Millay*; New York, 1945

Hedrick, Joan; *Harriet Beecher Stowe,A Life*; Oxford University Press, New York, 1994

Hopkins, Mary Ellen; *The It's Okay If You Sit On My Quilt Book*; ME Publications, Santa Monica, CA 1989

Jakovbek, Robert; *Harriet Beecher Stowe*; Chelsea House, New York, 1989

Jeffries, Ona Griffin; *In and Out of the White House*; Wilfred Funk, New York, 1960

Jensen, Amy; *The White House*; McGraw-Hill, New York, 1958

Johnston, Norma; *Louisa May*; Four Winds Press, New York, 1991

Keller, Helen; *My Religion*; Doubleday, Page & Co., New York, 1927

Klapthor, Margaret B.; *The First Ladies*; White House Historical Association, Washington, DC, 1975

Krass, Peter; *Sojourner Truth; Antislavery Activist*; Chelsea House, New York, 1988

Lash, Joseph P.; *Eleanor: The Years Alone;* Norton & Company, New York, 1972

Levin, Phyllis Lee; *Abigail Adams, A Biography*; Ballantine Books, New York, 1987

Lovric, Michelle; *Woman, An Illustrated Treasury*; Running Press, Philadelphia, 1993

Bibliography

McConnell, Jane & Burt; *Our First Ladies*; Crowell Company, New York, 1953

Meigs, Cornelia; *Invincible Louisa*; Little, Brown & Company, Boston, 1933

Ortiz, Victoria; *Sojourner Truth-A Self Made Woman*; Harper Collins, NY 1974

Prindiville, Kathleen; *First ladies, Stories of the Presidents' Wives*; McMillian Company, New York, 1964

Prindiville, Kathleen; *First Ladies*; MacMillian Co., New York, 1932

Read, Phyllis J. & Witlieb, Bernard; *The Book of Women's Firsts*; Random House, New York, 1992

Roosevelt, Eleanor; *My Day*; Pharos Books, New York, 1989

Roosevelt, Eleanor; *On My Own*; Harper & Brothers, New York, 1958

Roosevelt, Eleanor; *This I Remember*; Harper & Brothers, New York, 1949

Ross, Ishbel; *Grace Coolidge & Her Era*; Dodd, Mead & Co, New York, 1962

Sherr, Lynn; *Failure is Impossible*; Time Books, New York, 1995

Simon & Schuster; *A Treasury of American Heritage*; New York, 1954

Stetson, Erlene and David, Linda; *Glory in Tribulation*; Michigan State University Press, Michigan, 1994

Stibbs, Anne; *Words of Women*; Bloomsbury, London, 1993

Van Doren, Charles; *Websters American Biographies*; Massachusetts, 1975

Voss, Frederick; *The Smithsonian Treasury - The Presidents*; Randon House, New York, 1991

Washington, Margaret; *Narrative of Sojourner Truth*; Vintage Books, New York, 1993

Weatherford, Doris; *American Womens History*; Prentice Hall, New York, 1994

Webster, Marie D; *Quilts, Their Story and How to Make Them*; 1925

Whitney, Janet; *Abigail Adams*; Little Brown & Co., Boston, 1947

Wilson, Vincent, Jr.; *The Book of Distinguished American Woman*; American History Research Associates; Brookeville, Maryland, 1983

Wilson, Forest; *Crusade in Crinoline*; Lippencott Co, New York, 1941

Photo Credits

A'Lelia Bundles, Madam C.J. Walker photos

Library of Congress

Collection of the author

For further research on the women in this and the first volume I highly recommend the World Wide Web (Internet). There are many outstanding sites with multitudes of information about the women who helped shape the world we live in and are continuing to mold the future in which we will live.

About the Author

The author as a young terror.

Born and raised on a farm in Glasgow, Kentucky, Kaye now makes her home in Indianapolis, Indiana with her husband David. They have two children and six grand-children.

Kaye owns and operates two full service quilt shops and Bernina dealership locations of Quilt Quarters in Carmel and Indianapolis, Indiana. She is seminar coordinator for Mary Ellen Hopkins, designs fabric for South Sea Imports and has her own publishing company, Kaye England Publications.

Kaye began quiltmaking and fabric collecting in earnest in the early 1980's, but was influenced early on by a family of needleworkers. Kaye now travels around the world lecturing and teaching. She has previously published four books; *Voices of the Past*, *Journey to Jericho*, *Callie Lu's Sunflower* and *Winter Wonderland*.

Kaye has been described as a colorful individual generating enthusiasm and excitement in her work and having great fun in the process.

So many gods, so many creeds,
So many paths that wind and wind,
When just the art of being kind
Is all this sad world needs.
Ella Wheeler Wilcox